Jorge Luis Borges

Consulting Editors

Rodolfo Cardona
professor of Spanish
and comparative literature,
Boston University

James Cockcroft
visiting professor of Latin American
and Caribbean studies,
State University of New York at Albany

Hispanics of Achievement

Jorge Luis Borges

Adrian Lennon

Chelsea House Publishers
New York   Philadelphia

CHELSEA HOUSE PUBLISHERS

Editor-in-Chief: Remmel Nunn
Managing Editor: Karyn Gullen Browne
Copy Chief: Mark Rifkin
Picture Editor: Adrian G. Allen
Art Director: Maria Epes
Assistant Art Director: Noreen Romano
Manufacturing Manager: Gerald Levine
Systems Manager: Lindsey Ottman
Production Manager: Joseph Romano
Production Coordinator: Marie Claire Cebrián

Hispanics of Achievement
Senior Editor: John W. Selfridge

Staff for JORGE LUIS BORGES
Associate Editor: Philip Koslow
Copy Editor: Sol Liebowitz
Editorial Assistant: Martin Mooney
Designer: Robert Yaffe
Picture Researcher: Nisa Rauschenberg
Cover Illustration: Daniel Mark Duffy

3 5 7 9 8 6 4 2

Library of Congress Cataloging-in-Publication Data
Lennon, Adrian.
  Jorge Luis Borges/Adrian Lennon
    p. cm.—(Hispanics of achievement)
  Includes bibliographical references and index.
  Summary: Presents the life and times of the Argentine writer, in
text and photos.
  ISBN 0-7910-1236-0
       0-7910-1263-8 (pbk.)
  1. Borges, Jorge Luis 1899–1986—Juvenile literature. 2. Authors,
Argentine—20th century—Biography—Juvenile literature. [1. Bor-
ges, Jorge Luis,—1899–1986. 2. Authors, Argentine.] I. Title II.
Series
PQ7797.B635Z77344 1992   91-17667
868—dc20   CIP
  [B]   AC

Contents

Hispanics of Achievement

Oscar Arias Sánchez
Costa Rican president

Joan Baez
Mexican-American folksinger

Rubén Blades
Panamanian lawyer and entertainer

Jorge Luis Borges
Argentine writer

Juan Carlos
King of Spain

Pablo Casals
Spanish cellist and conductor

Miguel de Cervantes
Spanish writer

Cesar Chavez
Mexican-American labor leader

El Cid
Spanish military leader

Roberto Clemente
Puerto Rican baseball player

Plácido Domingo
Spanish singer

El Greco
Spanish artist

Gloria Estefan
Cuban-American singer

Gabriel García Márquez
Colombian writer

Raul Julia
Puerto Rican actor

José Martí
Cuban revolutionary and poet

Rita Moreno
Puerto Rican singer and actress

Pablo Neruda
Chilean poet and diplomat

Antonia Novello
U.S. surgeon general

Octavio Paz
Mexican poet and critic

Javier Pérez de Cuéllar
Peruvian diplomat

Anthony Quinn
Mexican-American actor

Diego Rivera
Mexican artist

Linda Ronstadt
Mexican-American singer

Antonio López de Santa Anna
Mexican general and politician

George Santayana
Spanish poet and philosopher

Junípero Serra
Spanish missionary and explorer

Lee Trevino
Mexican-American golfer

Pancho Villa
Mexican revolutionary

CHELSEA HOUSE PUBLISHERS

INTRODUCTION

Hispanics of Achievement

Rodolfo Cardona

The Spanish language and many other elements of Spanish culture are present in the United States today and have been since the country's earliest beginnings. Some of these elements have come directly from the Iberian Peninsula; others have come indirectly, by way of Mexico, the Caribbean basin, and the countries of Central and South America.

Spanish culture has influenced America in many subtle ways, and consequently many Americans remain relatively unaware of the extent of its impact. The vast majority of them recognize the influence of Spanish culture in America, but they often do not realize the great importance and long history of that influence. This is partly because Americans have tended to judge the Hispanic influence in the United States in statistical terms rather than to look closely at the ways in which individual Hispanics have profoundly affected American culture. For this reason, it is fitting that Americans obtain more than a passing acquaintance with the origins of these Spanish cultural elements and gain an understanding of how they have been woven into the fabric of American society.

It is well documented that Spanish seafarers were the first to explore and colonize many of the early territories of what is today called the United States of America. For this reason, students of geography discover Hispanic names all over the map of the United States. For instance, the Strait of Juan de Fuca was named after the Spanish explorer who first navigated the waters of the Pacific Northwest; the names of states such as Arizona (arid zone), Montana (mountain), Florida (thus named because it was reached on Easter Sunday, which in Spanish is called the feast of Pascua Florida), and California (named after a fictitious land in one of the first and probably the most popular among the Spanish novels of chivalry, *Amadis of Gaul*) are all derived from Spanish; and there are numerous mountains, rivers, canyons, towns, and cities with Spanish names throughout the United States.

Not only explorers but many other illustrious figures in Spanish history have helped define American culture. For example, the 13th-century king of Spain, Alfonso X, also known as the Learned, may be unknown to the majority of Americans, but his work on the codification of Spanish law has greatly influenced the evolution of American law, particularly in the jurisdictions of the Southwest. For this contribution a statue of him stands in the rotunda of the Capitol in Washington, D.C. Likewise, the name Diego Rivera may be unfamiliar to most Americans, but this Mexican painter influenced many American artists whose paintings, commissioned during the Great Depression and the New Deal era of the 1930s, adorn the walls of government buildings throughout the United States. In recent years the contributions of Puerto Ricans, Mexicans, Mexican Americans (Chicanos), and Cubans in American cities such as Boston, Chicago, Los Angeles, Miami, Minneapolis, New York, and San Antonio have been enormous.

The importance of the Spanish language in this vast cultural complex cannot be overstated. Spanish, after all, is second only to English as the most widely spoken of Western languages within the United States as well as in the entire world. The popularity of the Spanish language in America has a long history.

In addition to Spanish exploration of the New World, the great Spanish literary tradition served as a vehicle for bringing the language and culture to America. Interest in Spanish literature in America began when English immigrants brought with them translations of Spanish masterpieces of the Golden Age. As early as 1683, private libraries in Philadelphia and Boston contained copies of the first picaresque novel, *Lazarillo de Tormes*, translations of Francisco de Quevedo's *Los Sueños*, and copies of the immortal epic of reality and illusion *Don Quixote*, by the great Spanish writer Miguel de Cervantes. It would not be surprising if Cotton Mather, the arch-Puritan, read *Don Quixote* in its original Spanish, if only to enrich his vocabulary in preparation for his writing *La fe del cristiano en 24 artículos de la Institución de Cristo, enviada a los españoles para que abran sus ojos* (The Christian's Faith in 24 Articles of the Institution of Christ, Sent to the Spaniards to Open Their Eyes), published in Boston in 1699.

Over the years, Spanish authors and their works have had a vast influence on American literature—from Washington Irving, John Steinbeck, and Ernest Hemingway in the novel to Henry Wadsworth Longfellow and Archibald MacLeish in poetry. Such important American writers as James Fenimore Cooper, Edgar Allan Poe, Walt Whitman, Mark Twain, and Herman Melville all owe a sizable debt to the Spanish literary tradition. Some writers, such as Willa Cather and Maxwell Anderson, who explored Spanish themes they came into contact with in the American Southwest and Mexico, were influenced less directly but no less profoundly.

Important contributions to a knowledge of Spanish culture in the United States were also made by many lesser known individuals—teachers, publishers, historians, entrepreneurs, and others—with a love for Spanish culture. One of the most significant of these contributions was made by Abiel Smith, a Harvard College graduate of the class of 1764, when he bequeathed stock worth $20,000 to Harvard for the support of a professor of French and Spanish. By 1819 this endowment had produced enough income to appoint a professor, and the philologist and humanist George Ticknor became the first holder of the Abiel Smith Chair, which was the very first endowed Chair at Harvard University. Other illustrious holders of the Smith Chair would include the poets Henry Wadsworth Longfellow and James Russell Lowell.

A highly respected teacher and scholar, Ticknor was also a collector of Spanish books, and as such he made a very special contribution to America's knowledge of Spanish culture. He was instrumental in amassing for Harvard libraries one of the first and most impressive collections of Spanish books in the United States. He also had a valuable personal collection of Spanish books and manuscripts, which he bequeathed to the Boston Public Library.

With the creation of the Abiel Smith Chair, Spanish language and literature courses became part of the curriculum at Harvard, which also went on to become the first American university to offer graduate studies in Romance languages. Other colleges and universities throughout the United States gradually followed Harvard's example, and today Spanish language and culture may be studied at most American institutions of higher learning.

No discussion of the Spanish influence in the United States, however brief, would be complete without a mention of the Spanish influence on art. Important American artists such as John Singer Sargent, James A. M. Whistler, Thomas Eakins, and Mary Cassatt all explored Spanish subjects and experimented with Spanish techniques. Virtually every serious American artist living today has studied the work of the Spanish masters as well as the great 20th-century Spanish painters Salvador Dalí, Joan Miró, and Pablo Picasso.

The most pervasive Spanish influence in America, however, has probably been in music. Compositions such as Leonard Bernstein's *West Side Story*, the Latinization of William Shakespeare's *Romeo and Juliet* set in New York's Puerto Rican quarter, and Aaron Copland's *Salon Mexico* are two obvious examples. In general, one can hear the influence of Latin rhythms—from tango to mambo, from guaracha to salsa—in virtually every form of American music.

This series of biographies, which Chelsea House has published under the general title HISPANICS OF ACHIEVEMENT, constitutes further recognition of—and a renewed effort to bring forth to the consciousness of America's young people—the contributions that Hispanic people have made not only in the United States but throughout the civilized world. The men and women who are featured in this series have attained a high level of accomplishment in their respective fields of endeavor and have made a permanent mark on American society.

The title of this series must be understood in its broadest possible sense: The term *Hispanics* is intended to include Spaniards, Spanish Americans, and individuals from many countries whose language and culture have either direct or indirect Spanish origins. The names of many of the people included in this series will be immediately familiar; others will be less recognizable. All, however, have attained recognition within their own countries, and often their fame has transcended their borders.

The series HISPANICS OF ACHIEVEMENT thus addresses the attainments and struggles of Hispanic people in the United States and seeks to tell the stories of individuals whose personal and professional lives in some way reflect the larger Hispanic experience. These stories are exemplary of what human beings can accomplish, often against daunting odds and by extraordinary personal sacrifice, where there is conviction and determination. Fray Junípero Serra, the 18th-century Spanish Franciscan missionary, is one such individual. Although in very poor health, he devoted the last 15 years of his life to the foundation of missions throughout California—then a mostly unsettled expanse of land—in an effort to bring a better life to Native Americans through the cultivation of crafts and animal husbandry. An example from recent times, the Mexican-American labor leader Cesar Chavez has battled bitter opposition and made untold personal sacrifices in his effort to help poor agricultural workers who have been exploited for decades on farms throughout the Southwest.

The talent with which each one of these men and women may have been endowed required dedication and hard work to develop and become fully realized. Many of them have enjoyed rewards for their efforts during their own lifetime, whereas others have died poor and unrecognized. For some it took a long time to achieve their goals, for others success came at an early age, and for still others the struggle continues. All of them, however, stand out as people whose lives have made a difference, whose achievements we need to recognize today and should continue to honor in the future.

Jorge Luis Borges

Jorge Luis Borges, photographed during a visit to the University of Texas in 1962. One of Argentina's leading writers since the 1920s, Borges achieved worldwide recognition when he won the International Publishers Prize in 1961.

CHAPTER ONE

In Search of Borges

In October 1982, the Swedish Academy in Stockholm awarded the Nobel Prize in literature to the Colombian novelist Gabriel García Márquez, best known for his novel *Cien años de soledad* (One Hundred Years of Solitude). García Márquez was naturally overjoyed at receiving the world's most prestigious literary prize. But he took the opportunity to wonder aloud why the Nobel Prize had not been awarded to a different Latin American writer. "I hope he receives it," García Márquez remarked to reporters who flocked to interview him, "and I still don't understand why they haven't given it to him." He was talking about Jorge Luis Borges.

At the time, Jorge Luis Borges was living in Buenos Aires, Argentina. He was 83 years old, and he had been blind since the mid-1950s. If he felt slighted because he had been passed over for the Nobel Prize, he gave no indication to the public. He was accustomed to being overlooked when it came to honors. Although he had written his most brilliant short stories during the 1930s and 1940s, he was unknown outside Latin America until 1961, when he won the International Publishers Prize. By the end of the decade his books were everywhere, and he was finally recognized as one of the masters of modern literature.

Despite his fame, Borges remained a puzzle to many readers and students of literature. On the one hand, he had almost invented a new form of writing—the short story that explored philosophical questions about the nature of reality. The element of fantasy in his work had clearly inspired the "magic realism" that critics hailed in the work of younger Latin American writers, such as García Márquez, Isabel Allende, Julio Cortázar, Mario Vargas Llosa, and Carlos Fuentes. These writers themselves always acknowledged their debt to Borges. As early as the 1960s, Fuentes had written, "Without Borges's prose there simply would not be a modern Spanish-American novel."

But Borges differed from the younger generation by avoiding political and social issues, which he did not consider proper subjects for literature. As a private individual, he had always believed passionately in liberty and justice. He had, for example, vigorously opposed the Argentine dictator Juan Perón during the 1940s and 1950s. As a result, Borges lost his job and was threatened with death. Although he emerged from this ordeal a hero to many Argentines, it had no obvious effect on his writing.

In 1976, when Argentina came under the sway of a military dictatorship, Borges upset many of his admirers by supporting the ruling generals. He did, however, lend his support to those protesting the fate of los Desaparecidos (the Disappeared Ones), opponents of the regime who were being jailed, tortured, and killed by the thousands. In 1982, Borges broke entirely with the regime after Argentina seized the British-held Falkland Islands (Islas Malvinas), in the southwestern Atlantic Ocean, resulting in what Borges termed an "absurd war" with Great Britain and a resounding military defeat for Argentina. No one can say with certainty, but it is quite possible that Borges's political attitudes cost him a chance at the Nobel Prize.

Upon winning the 1982 Nobel Prize in literature, the Colombian novelist Gabriel García Márquez paid tribute to Borges. "I hope he receives [the Nobel Prize]," García Márquez stated, "and I still don't understand why they haven't given it to him."

"I don't understand my own country," he admitted to an interviewer in 1982. Then he added, in classic Borgesian style, "But the world is not meant to be understood by men. Every night, I dream. I have nightmares—of being lost, of being in an unknown city. I don't remember the name of the hotel, or I can't find my way home in Buenos Aires. Maybe I feel very lost because the world is meaningless."

The search for meaning, the feeling of being lost in the universe, were themes that had haunted Borges all his life. He was accustomed to questioning everyday realities, even the fact of his own existence. Indeed, if the Swedish Academy had wished to award the Nobel Prize to Borges, a reading of his story "Borges and I" might have caused them to wonder how to find the right person.

> It's to the other man, to Borges, that things happen. I walk along the streets of Buenos Aires, stopping now and then— perhaps out of habit—to look at the arch of an old entrance-way or a grillwork gate; of Borges I get news through the mail and glimpse his name among a committee of professors or in a dictionary of biography. . . . I live, I let myself live, so that Borges can weave his tales and poems, and those tales and poems are my justification. . . . I am fated to become lost once and for all, and only some moment

of myself will survive in the other man. Little by little, I have been surrendering everything to him, even though I have evidence of his stubborn habit of falsification and exaggerating.

The story concludes with the line "Which of us is writing this page I don't know." Many artists have undoubtedly felt that they express themselves more fully in their work than in their everyday life. But few have suggested that there is a war between the self that lives from day to day and the self that creates the work of art. Few have explored the feeling that life is a journey through a labyrinth, or maze—a theme that occurs over and over in Borges's work—and that every turning may reveal a mirror in which one will see an unrecognizable image. Borges in many ways based his career as a writer on just such a feeling.

Was he, then, at the age of 82, simply an old man depressed by blindness, confused by the world around him, and no longer interested in life? The Borges who wrote may have given the impression that he must be. But the Borges who lived in Buenos Aires was an entirely different person, still filled with ideas and youthful energy. Willis Barnstone, a poet and professor of literature at Indiana University, visited Borges in 1975 and had a memorable walk with him through the streets of Buenos Aires:

The British destroyer HMS Sheffield *after being struck by an Argentine missile during the 1982 Falklands War. Argentina's attempt to seize the British-held Falkland Islands ended in a humiliating defeat for Argentina. Borges, who had previously supported the government, condemned the war as "absurd."*

As the hours passed Borges seemed to be more and more
awake to every oddity in the streets, to the architecture
which his blind eyes somehow knew, to the few passersby. . .
At first I thought he might not know his way [back to his
apartment], for he stopped every few steps when he made
some important point and circled about as if we were lost.
But no, he wanted to talk about his sister Nora and their
childhood, about the black man he saw shot on the Brazil-
Uruguay border some forty years earlier, about his military
ancestors who fought in the civil wars of the nineteenth century. Often his cane would hit against a hole or small ditch
in the broken pavement, and each small event offered him
the chance to pause, to stretch his cane and to extend his
arms and legs in the posture of an actor. . . . By dawn we
reached his building.

The American writer Paul Theroux, visiting Buenos Aires a few
years later, had occasion to observe how Borges was regarded by his
fellow citizens: "The restaurant was full this Good Friday night, and
it was extremely noisy. But as soon as Borges entered, tapping his
cane, feeling his way through the tables he obviously knew well,
a hush fell upon the diners. Borges was recognized, and at his
entrance all talking and eating ceased. It was both a reverential and
curious silence, and it was maintained until Borges took his seat
and gave the waiter our order."

Theroux also found Borges to be a tireless companion, eager to
stay up late talking and having someone read to him. At these
moments, the Borges who lived and the Borges who wrote were
perhaps as close to being at peace with one another as they ever
could be. But for those who can only approach Borges through his
writing, there will always be an element of mystery about him. The
search for his identity is not unlike a trip through one of those
labyrinths that so fired his imagination. When the going becomes
difficult, it may be helpful to remember Borges's words: "I believe
that in the idea of the labyrinth there is also hope, or salvation."

*This German engraving depicts a scene from the early European explora-
tion of the New World—the arrest of Christopher Columbus in 1500 on
the island of Hispaniola. Columbus's discoveries paved the way for the
Spanish settlement of Argentina in 1516, and Borges's ancestors were
among the first Argentines.*

CHAPTER TWO

Palermo

Jorge Luis Borges was born in Argentina's capital, Buenos Aires, on August 24, 1899. At the time of his birth, his parents lived in the heart of the city, but shortly afterward the family moved to Palermo, a rather shabby suburb on the northern outskirts. The very name of this district—derived from the capital of Sicily, Italy—says a great deal about Argentina's society at the time of Borges's birth and about the varied influences on his intellectual development.

Since its settlement by Spain in 1516, the population of Argentina had consisted largely of Spaniards, native Indians, and people of mixed Spanish and Indian heritage, known as mestizos. By the middle of the 19th century, mestizos accounted for more than 500,000 of Argentina's approximately 800,000 inhabitants. At this point, the government decided that the future of the country would be best secured if Europeans were to outnumber the mestizos and thus become the ruling group. The government began to encourage massive emigration from Europe, principally from Italy and Spain: Italians and Spaniards made up four-fifths of the

6 million immigrants who came to Argentina between 1844 and 1914. Thus the country in which Borges was born was rapidly becoming a crossroads of New World and Old World cultures.

Borges himself, like many other Argentines, had a diverse ancestry. He could count among his forebears both the Portuguese sailors who had been the first to discover the territory that became Argentina and the Spanish conquistadores who settled the country. (Borges is a name with Portuguese roots.) More specifically, he was descended from Juan de Garay, the man who founded the seaport of Buenos Aires in 1580; Hernando Arias de Saavedra, who introduced into Argentina one of the nation's economic staples— cattle—and played a crucial role in the settling of the Río de la Plata region; and Jerónimo Luis de Cabrera y Garay, who became governor of Río de la Plata in 1641. His later ancestors, with whom Borges would chiefly identify, were equally important figures in Argentine history. Francisco Narciso de Laprida presided over the Congress of Tucumán, which in 1816 declared Argentina's independence from Spain, and Colonel Isidoro Suárez fought in the war of independence. Isidoro de Acevedo Laprida fought in the civil war against Juan Manuel de Rosas, Argentina's legendary 19th-century tyrant, and Justo José de Urquiza aided in the final defeat of Rosas in 1852. The home of Borges's maternal grandfather, Isidoro de Acevedo Laprida, in which Borges was born, was almost a family museum. The house was filled with swords that had been used in the wars of liberation, carefully preserved uniforms, and velvet-framed photographs of heroic freedom fighters. The images of his ancestors and the tales of their exploits remained with Borges always: The question of physical bravery and the clash between the violence of the Argentine frontier and the European culture of the cities are themes to which he returned again and again in his stories.

Equally important to Borges's literary background was the figure of his grandmother, Fanny Haslam de Borges, who had been born in Staffordshire, England. As a young woman, Fanny Haslam

Colonels Isidoro Suárez (left) and Francisco Borges were among Jorge Luis Borges's heroic forebears. Borges was born in a house filled with military souvenirs, and although he was destined to live by the pen rather than by the sword, the theme of personal bravery appears often in his writing.

came to Argentina to live with her eldest sister, who had married Jorge Suárez, an Italian-Jewish engineer who introduced horse-drawn tram cars to Argentina during the 19th century. In about 1870, Haslam married Francisco Borges, a colonel in the Argentine army. They settled in Argentina's frontier provinces, where Colonel Borges was killed at the age of 41 during one of Argentina's frequent civil wars. Fanny Haslam de Borges ran a boardinghouse after her husband's death and lived to the age of 90; in addition to entertaining her grandson with tales of life on the frontier, she was responsible for his knowledge of the English language and his early enthusiasm for English literature. When Borges was a child, his grandmother often read to him from English magazines and saw to it that his early education was supervised by an English governess, Miss Tink. The mixture of Spanish and English in the household was so complete that for a long time the young Jorge—called Georgie by the family—did not even realize that they were separate languages. As he explained to an interviewer in 1973: "When I was talking to my paternal grandmother I had to speak in a manner that I afterward discovered was called English, and when I was talking to my mother or her parents I had to talk a language that turned out to be Spanish."

Fanny Haslam de Borges had given birth to two sons before the death of her husband. Her elder son became an officer in the Argentine navy, and her younger son—Jorge Guillermo, Borges's father—became a lawyer with a passion for poetry and philosophy. Jorge Guillermo Borges had a powerful impact on his son's development. Although a successful professional, he was hardly a conventional man. The elder Borges considered himself an anarchist, one who believed that human beings could manage their affairs without the need for governments, armies, police, or organized religion. "Once," Borges later wrote, "he told me that I should take a good look at soldiers, uniforms, barracks, flags, churches, priests, and butcher shops, since all these things were about to disappear, and I could tell my children that I had actually seen them. The prophecy has not yet come true, unfortunately."

In addition to his work as a lawyer, the elder Borges taught psychology—a new field of study at the beginning of the 20th century—at the Normal School for Modern Languages in Buenos Aires. At home, he taught his young son the basics of philosophy. Using a chessboard, the elder Borges demonstrated the intriguing puzzles posed by Zeno of Elea, a Greek philosopher who lived during the 5th century B.C. Zeno delighted in standing truth on its head by the strict use of logic. He argued, for example, that Achilles, the legendary Greek warrior, could never beat a tortoise in a race if the tortoise had a head start. This was so because Achilles first had to cover the distance between his own starting point and the starting point of the tortoise. While Achilles was doing this, the tortoise would also advance a certain distance. Then Achilles would have to cover the added distance while the tortoise advanced again, and this process would go on forever, so that Achilles could never overtake the tortoise. In real life, of course, any average human can beat a tortoise in a race; but as Borges's father enacted the contest with two chess pieces, Zeno's argument could not be refuted. It was proof to young Georgie that the power of the human mind could overcome everyday reality.

When Borges was two years old, his family moved to this house in the Palermo district of Buenos Aires. Borges later recalled that when the neighbors sat outside on warm evenings, "the street was cozy and light and the empty houses were like lanterns in a row."

In addition to his love of philosophy, Jorge Guillermo Borges had a passion for books. As Borges wrote in his "Autobiographical Essay," published in 1970: "If I were asked to name the chief event in my life, I should say my father's library. In fact, I sometimes think I have never strayed outside that library. I can still picture it. It was in a room of its own, with glass-fronted shelves, and must have contained several thousand volumes." The first books Georgie read were by British and American authors with a taste for mystery and adventure—Mark Twain, Edgar Allan Poe, H. G. Wells, Robert Louis Stevenson. He also read English translations of the great Spanish classic *Don Quixote*, as well as *Grimm's Fairy Tales* and *The Thousand and One Nights*. In Spanish, he read about the outlaws of the Argentine frontier and the exploits of his military ancestors.

Like many young boys, Georgie dreamed of being a military hero, but the example of his father exerted more power over him than the swords and uniforms displayed in the family home. Jorge Guillermo Borges had published poems, stories, and a novel, but before long his failing eyesight prevented him from enjoying a full-fledged literary career. "From the time I was a boy," Borges recalled, " . . . it was tacitly understood that I had to fulfill the literary destiny that circumstances had denied my father. This was something that was taken for granted (and such things are far more important than things that are merely said). I was expected to be a writer."

Borges later believed that he began writing at the age of six or seven. His first efforts were understandably clumsy, but his father never criticized them, preferring to let young Georgie correct his

Fanny Haslam, Borges's English-born grandmother, in a photograph taken shortly before her marriage to Colonel Francisco Borges. After her husband was killed in battle, Haslam stayed in Argentina and raised her two sons. She maintained her English ways and instilled in her grandson a great love of the language.

own mistakes. This technique was obviously the right one, because when Georgie was nine years old, a Spanish translation of a story by the British writer Oscar Wilde appeared in *El País* (The Nation), a Buenos Aires newspaper. The translation was signed Jorge Borges, and everyone naturally assumed that it had been done by Georgie's father. In fact, it had been done by Georgie himself.

It may appear that Georgie became an adult long before his time, but he did enjoy some childish pursuits. He had a passion for the Buenos Aires zoo and was especially fascinated by the more ferocious animals. As he told an interviewer during the early 1980s, "I used to stop for a long time in front of the tiger's cage to see him pacing back and forth. I liked his natural beauty, his black stripes and his golden stripes. And now that I am blind, one single color remains for me, and it is precisely the color of the tiger, the color yellow." At times, Georgie became so engrossed in the tiger and the other animals that his mother could only get him to leave by threatening to take away all his books.

Even at home, when Georgie played with his sister, Norah, two years younger than he, their games had a literary quality. According to an account published by Alicia Jurado in 1964, based on an interview with Norah, "He liked to reenact with her scenes taken from books: he was a prince and she the queen, his mother; standing on a staircase, they leaned over to hear the acclamations of an imaginary multitude; or they traveled to the moon in a missile made by folding a red silk Chinese screen, embroidered with golden birds and flowers, into which they tumbled after sliding down the banister of the staircase. Sometimes, they traveled dangerously on the flat roofs, searching for a room where they'd never been."

Another world that Borges came to know early in life was the neighboring country of Uruguay, which shared a great deal of history with Argentina. Georgie's mother was part Uruguayan, and her cousin Francisco Haedo owned a villa on the outskirts of the capital city, Montevideo, in a rural village called Paso Molino. In the summertime, the Borgeses often made the 12-hour ferry trip across the wide, muddy Río de la Plata and paid an extended visit to the Haedos. Georgie and Norah allowed their cousin Esther Haedo, who had also been educated by an English governess, to join in their games. Often the children went to an old wooden lookout tower on the Haedo property; there the two girls defended Georgie against an imaginary enemy who was out to murder him. The game became so real to them that one day when they were in the house taking a nap, they were terrified by the reflection of the imaginary murderer in a wardrobe mirror. Mirrors retained a lifelong fascination for Borges and figured in many of his stories; the image of two mirrors endlessly reflecting each other became for him a symbol of the mystery of the universe.

The Haedos also owned a ranch near Fray Bentos, on the Uruguay River, and the family spent part of the summer there. Borges learned to swim in the swift, treacherous currents of the Uruguay, becoming an unusually strong swimmer in an age in which swimming was not a common pursuit. (When he asked some

Borges and his younger sister, Norah, at the Buenos Aires zoo in 1908. Although Borges preferred reading to all other activities, he was fascinated by wild animals. Often, his mother could get him to leave the zoo only by threatening to take away his books.

cowboys if they knew how to swim, they replied scornfully, "Water is for cattle.") He also discovered for himself the pampas, the South American plains where his English grandmother had spent most of her married life. Here Georgie gathered impressions and legends that would later be shaped into stories of battles, duels, and desperate crimes. One of his most memorable tales, "The Story of the Warrior and the Captive," drew directly on his grandmother's encounter with an Englishwoman who had lived among the Indians for 15 years: "Perhaps the two women felt for an instant as if

A group of gauchos, Argentine cowboys, herd sheep on the pampas, the vast plains of Argentina. The gauchos were known for their independent spirit and their love of knife fighting; the legends of their exploits made a deep impression on the young Borges and later inspired some of his best stories.

they were sisters, here in this incredible land far from their own beloved island. My grandmother said something; the other answered with difficulty, searching for the words and repeating them as if astonished by an ancient savor. . . . She said that she was from Yorkshire, that her parents had emigrated to Buenos Aires, that she had lost them in an Indian raid, that the Indians had carried her off, and that now she was the wife of a chieftain to whom she had already given two sons and who was very brave." Borges's grandmother urged the woman to stay in the settlements and promised to bring her children to her, but the woman disappeared:

> Nevertheless, they saw each other once more. My grandmother had gone out hunting; on a ranch, near the sheepdip, a man was cutting the throat of a sheep. As if in a dream, the Indian woman came by on a horse. She threw herself to the ground and drank the warm blood. I don't know whether she did this because she could no longer act differently or as a challenge and a sign.

Georgie's carefree life took a sharp turn in 1908, when he began to attend a state-run school. Previously, his parents had kept him out of school because they feared he would catch a deadly childhood disease. In addition, his father distrusted all government enterprises and disliked the religious instruction that was so much a part of public education. However, there were limits to how much Georgie could learn from Miss Tink, and at the age of nine, he ventured out into the wider world of classrooms and classmates.

School was not a happy experience. Georgie had to wear glasses because of his poor eyesight, and his classmates taunted him. In addition, he dressed in the English style, wearing a short jacket and high collar; this was natural for a child of his background but unusual in Buenos Aires, where the cultural model was predominantly French and the British were often resented for their economic domination of Argentina. As a result, Georgie often found himself goaded into fights. He was not especially strong or skilled with his fists, but he always accepted a challenge. The code of the duel had been bred into him by tales of his ancestors' exploits. He could not allow himself to be seen as a coward. As a result, he absorbed a number of beatings at the hands of his fellow students, whom he remembered as "amateur hooligans."

Despite his unhappiness, Georgie did well at history, literature, and philosophy. At the same time, he continued to learn from his father at home. Not surprisingly, considering his experiences at school, he shared his father's belief that English was superior to Spanish and that Argentine culture was hopelessly backward. If Georgie had simply stayed in Argentina, he might have held those opinions for the rest of his life. But a sudden decision by his father gave Georgie a new perspective of the world.

Jorge Luis Borges and his sister, Norah (left, front), attended high school in Geneva, Switzerland, from 1914 to 1918. The school required them to learn French; Georgie had a difficult time mastering the new language, but Norah picked it up so well that she even dreamed in French.

CHAPTER THREE

The European

In the summer of 1914, Jorge Guillermo Borges decided to retire from his legal practice and take his family to Europe. The immediate reason for this decision was his failing eyesight, the result of a hereditary disorder that would eventually afflict his son as well. Borges remembered his father saying, with perfect logic, "How on earth can I sign my name to legal papers when I am unable to read them?"

Once the decision was made to leave Argentina, preparations for the journey took only 10 days. At that time, the borders of all countries were open to everyone, and travelers did not have to worry about obtaining passports and visas. The Borgeses were not wealthy, but in those days the Argentine peso was strong, and what money they had would go a long way in Europe. As Emir Rodriguez Monegal explains in his book *Jorge Luis Borges: A Literary Biography*: "Those were the years when landowners in Argentina, made rich by the meat and dairy products of their ranches, used to spend a great part of their fortune in Europe; when European elegance was carefully copied on both banks of the River Plate; and when the wealthy journeyed to Europe with their servants and sometimes even with their favorite cows."

The Borgeses did not take any servants or cows with them to Europe, but they did take Georgie's maternal grandmother, Leonor Suárez de Acevedo. The plan was for Georgie and Norah to stay in Geneva, Switzerland, with their grandmother while their parents took a tour of the Continent. After a few months, the family would return to Argentina. There was only one hitch in this plan: In August 1914, the nations of Europe became embroiled in the First World War, which was to last until 1918.

The war took the Borgeses completely by surprise. From the standpoint of the late 20th century, it may seem incredible that they were unaware of the conflicts brewing between the Triple Entente (England, France, and Russia) and the Central Powers (Germany and Austria-Hungary). But Argentina was a long way from Europe, and there was no television or radio to bring instant reports of events in other parts of the world. There were books and newspapers, to be sure, but Argentina at this time was a nation preoccupied with its own affairs. In his "Autobiographical Essay," Borges complains about the narrow focus of the school he attended in Buenos Aires: "My father used to say that Argentine history had taken the place of the catechism, so we were expected to worship all things Argentine. We were taught Argentine history, for example, before we were allowed any knowledge of the many lands and many centuries that went into its making." In addition, there had been no major military conflict in Europe since the Franco-Prussian War of 1870; economic prosperity and the opening of frontiers had convinced many others besides the Borgeses that the world was entering a new era of harmony. That dream was shattered in August 1914.

The elder Borgeses were in Germany when the war broke out. They managed to find their way to Geneva, where they remained for the duration of the war. Switzerland was a neutral country, so

Borges's parents, Jorge Guillermo Borges and Leonor Acevedo de Borges. Because of failing eyesight, Borges's father decided to give up his law practice and take his family to Europe. As her husband became increasingly blind, Leonor Borges gradually became the mainstay of the family.

the Borgeses were relatively safe, if somewhat isolated, within its
borders. The isolation was relieved somewhat when Fanny Haslam
de Borges, nearly 70 but still filled with the courage that had
impelled her to set out for Argentina as a young woman, decided
that she missed her family too much to stay in Buenos Aires.
Braving the German submarines that were prowling the Atlantic,
she sailed to Europe and rejoined the Borgeses in Geneva. In 1916,
a few of the Haedo cousins also made the journey. Georgie had
missed his grandmother, but Emir Rodriguez Monegal, after ex-
amining a photograph of him surrounded by nine female relatives,
wondered if the large-scale family reunion was not a mixed bless-

A German machine gun company in action during World War I. Borges's parents
were in Germany when the war began in August 1914. They managed to rejoin their
children in neutral Switzerland, where they remained in safety until the war ended
in 1918.

ing: "Even with his closest relatives he seems the odd man out, the stranger. The difference is visible in the expression of the face, the sadness of the eyes behind the thick glasses, and the terribly unhappy mouth. It is also evident in the way he sits or stands, always so clumsily, as if his body, growing too quickly and with a will of its own, bothered him too much."

It is difficult to know whether Borges was happy or unhappy in Geneva. The isolation and the damp, chilly climate were certainly a shock to him after the sunshine and the wide-open spaces of Argentina. Writing in 1927, he recalled: "I spent the war years in Geneva; a no-exit time, tight, made of drizzle, which I'll always remember with some hatred." However, after revisiting Geneva during the 1980s, he wrote of it in a totally different spirit.

> Of all the cities on the planet, of all the divine and intimate places which a man seeks out and merits in the course of his voyages, Geneva strikes me as the most propitious for happiness. . . . Unlike other cities, Geneva is not emphatic. Paris does not ignore that it is Paris, decorous London knows that it is London. But Geneva scarcely knows that it is Geneva.

In other words, Geneva did not impose itself on Georgie, it did not dazzle him with its beauty or sweep him up in its rhythm. It gave him a chance to grow and experiment, to develop the European side of his heritage and sort out his feelings about Argentina.

The Borgeses' apartment was in the city's old quarter, near the Collège Calvin, the high school where Georgie was to study for four years. Before Georgie could enroll, however, he had to study French with a private teacher and then at an academy, because French was the language in which classes at the Collège Calvin were conducted. This was Georgie's third language and the first to give him difficulty. His sister, Norah, had an easier time, learning French so well she even dreamed in it. "I remember my mother's coming home one day," Borges later wrote, "and finding Norah hidden behind a red plush curtain, crying out in fear, *'Une mouche,*

A view of Geneva, with Lake Geneva in the foreground and the Alps in the background. As a teenager, Borges found the city cold and dreary, but in later years he wrote: "Of all the cities on the planet, . . . Geneva strikes me as the most propitious for happiness."

une mouche!' ['A fly, a fly!'] It seems she had adopted the French notion that flies are dangerous. 'You come out of there,' my mother told her, somewhat unpatriotically. 'You were born and bred among flies!'"

Georgie began attending the Collège Calvin in the fall of 1914. Of the 40 or so students in his class, half were non-Swiss. The principal subject was Latin, but Georgie also studied algebra, chemistry, physics, botany, and zoology. By the end of his first year, despite the difficulty of studying every subject in French, a language he had hardly mastered, Georgie managed to pass all his exams—except the French examination itself. His classmates—with whom Georgie had become popular, a delightful and encouraging surprise after his depressing experience at the state school in Buenos Aires—banded together and asked the headmaster to consider the unusual effort and progress Georgie had made. The headmaster was moved by the request and advanced Georgie to the next grade.

Not surprisingly, Georgie felt most powerfully drawn to the students who came from abroad. His best friends at school were

Simon Jichlinski and Maurice Abramowicz, both of Polish-Jewish descent. Georgie taught them *truco*, an Argentine card game based on shifting alliances between players, alliances created by subtle and mysterious signals. Truco was the only card game Georgie ever liked—he described it as "a game whose real aim is to pass time with mischief and verses"—and his friends took to it so well that they cleaned him out the very first time they played. Having grown up in Europe, Jichlinski and Abramowicz were more sophisticated than Georgie, both in the ways of European life and the range of their reading. Among other things, they introduced him to the 19th-century Symbolist poets of France, principally Paul Verlaine, Arthur Rimbaud, and Stéphane Mallarmé. The Symbolists had rejected the idea of trying to describe the world in realistic detail. Instead, they wished to capture the inner life of human beings, depicting ideas, emotions, and impressions with striking symbols. They were not afraid of confusing the reader, because they believed that truth was cloaked in mystery. This was a great departure from the literature Georgie had been used to, and the influence of the Symbolist approach is clear in his later writing. It is also significant that Jichlinski and Abramowicz, who became a doctor and a lawyer, respectively, remained Borges's friends for life. They never lost touch with one another after Borges left Geneva, even though they were not to meet again until the early 1970s. And when they were reunited, Borges recalled, "We talked, we went on talking without minding the fact that half a century had elapsed, about the same things, the French Symbolists. It was a very fine experience. No word was said about the interim."

Borges also continued his readings in English. Among the British authors he discovered at this time was Thomas Carlyle (1795–1881), who pioneered a technique that Georgie was to use a number of times later in his career. The idea was to avoid writing a whole book to develop an idea that could really be expressed in just a few pages. Why not just pretend that a book had already been written and then write a short review of it? The idea could be

The Collège Calvin, where Borges attended high school. Borges was very popular with his classmates; when he failed his French examination at the end of the first year, the other students convinced the headmaster to advance him to the next grade.

explored, and then both reader and writer would be free to move on. Of course, there was always the danger that some readers would be confused and go off looking for books that had never been published. But as far as Carlyle and Georgie were concerned, that only added to the charm of the work.

In 1918, Georgie's maternal grandmother, Leonor Suárez de Acevedo, died, and the Borgeses moved east from Geneva to Lugano, where they remained for a year. At this time, all of Europe was suffering from a shortage of food as a result of the war, and Georgie experienced hunger for the first time. But as he later wrote, more pleasant memories of Lugano remained with him: "One of them is a morning, not overly cold, in November 1918, when my father and I read on a slate board in an almost deserted plaza the chalk words announcing the surrender of the Central Empires, that is: the desired peace. We returned to the hotel and broke the good news (there was no radiotelephone as yet) and drank toasts, not of champagne but of Italian red."

By 1919, life in Europe began to resume its normal pattern, and the Borgeses were finally free to return home. Before doing so, they decided to visit Spain. They took a train to Barcelona and continued on by boat to the beautiful island of Majorca, where Georgie impressed the natives with his ability as a swimmer. In the winter of 1919, the Borgeses moved to Seville in southwestern Spain, a city with a great historical and literary tradition.

During the great age of exploration in the 15th and 16th centuries, when mariners and conquistadores had sailed off to the New World, Seville had been their base of operations. But it was not the storied past of Seville that appealed to the 20-year-old Borges. He was far more interested in meeting young people who shared his passion for literature. He found this more difficult than he had expected.

> In Seville, I fell in with the literary group formed around [the magazine] *Grecia*. This group, who called themselves ultraists, had set out to renew literature, a branch of the arts about which they knew nothing whatever. . . . It baffled my Argentine mind to learn that they had no French and no inkling at all that such a thing as English literature existed . . . . As for *Grecia* itself, the editor, Isaac del Vando Villar, had the whole corpus of his poetry written for him by one or another of his assistants. I remember one of them telling me one day, "I'm very busy—Isaac is writing a poem."

Borges had much better luck when the family moved to Madrid, the capital of Spain. There he met Rafael Cansinos-Asséns, a 36-year-old poet and scholar who spoke 11 languages. Cansinos was an unusual man in many ways. According to Borges, Cansinos had originally studied for the priesthood but changed his plans when he read some historical documents that listed Cansinos as a Jewish name. Cansinos immediately declared himself a Jew, began to study Hebrew, and eventually underwent the Jewish rite of circumcision. This was a very extreme form of behavior in Spain, from which both Jews and Muslims had been expelled in 1492. Ever since then, Spaniards had been accustomed to boast of their pure Spanish blood and staunch Catholicism. Cansinos's decision to turn his back on this heritage was to be echoed in Borges's own actions during the 1930s, when he took a stand against the anti-Jewish sentiments emerging in Europe and Argentina.

Borges found in Cansinos the role model he had been searching for. Here was a man of genuine talent who was totally dedicated to literature, caring nothing for money or fame. According to Borges, Cansinos's entire house was a library; visitors had to thread their way through columns of books that rose from the floor and reached all the way to the ceiling. Borges later wrote, "Cansinos seemed to me as if he were all the past of that Europe I was leaving behind—something like the symbol of all culture, Western and Eastern."

Cansinos was the leader of a group that gathered every Saturday night at Madrid's Café Colonial. At times as many as 20 or 30 people would show up, and they would stay up all night discussing literature. They called themselves ultraists, another way of saying that they meant to go as far as possible in finding new ways to

Stéphane Mallarmé (1842–98), a leader of the French Symbolist movement, which revolutionized modern poetry. The Symbolists were a favorite topic of discussion for Borges and his schoolmates, and Symbolist poetry had a lifelong influence on his own writing.

express their thoughts and feelings. (*Ultra* is the Latin word for "beyond.") In this attitude, they were very much in tune with young people throughout the world who had lost all faith in their elders during the war years, when millions of young men were slaughtered on the battlefields of Europe. The staid, solemn forms that had prevailed in both society and literature were gone for good. In Russia, the Bolshevik party had seized power in the October Revolution of 1917, founding a government that for the first time in history claimed to draw its power solely from the workers and peasants. Inspired by this upheaval, young writers refused to copy the carefully worked out novels and poems of the prewar years, when everything had a beginning, a middle, and an end. Instead, they followed the French Symbolists and tried to mirror the life within and around them, recording vivid, jagged impressions, often putting things on paper without trying to make sense of them. Borges, having been taught by his father to despise armies and governments and having witnessed—fortunately from a safe vantage point—the horror and stupidity of war, was more than happy to support the October Revolution and to call himself an ultraist.

With the inspiration of Cansinos and his followers, Borges produced two books while in Spain. One was a collection of essays on literature and politics, the other a collection of poems, a few of which were published in the magazines *Grecia* and *Ultra* during 1920 and 1921. Looking back, Borges dismissed both books as essentially worthless; he must have adopted that attitude soon after writing them, because he destroyed both manuscripts before leaving for Buenos Aires in March 1921. Despite his self-criticism, he had made enormous strides during his years in Europe. First, he had completely absorbed the European culture that was a major part of his heritage. Equally important, he had ended his visit by rediscovering the Spanish language, in which he was to write exclusively for the rest of his life. Whether he knew it or not, at the age of 21, Borges had already absorbed all the ingredients for the work that was to bring him worldwide fame.

A view of Congallo Street in downtown Buenos Aires, photographed in 1924. (Mitchell's Book Store, a favorite of Borges's father, is in the left foreground.) When Borges returned from Europe, he found the capital bustling with cultural activity.

CHAPTER FOUR

Return of the Native

When he returned to Buenos Aires, the 21-year-old Borges saw his native city with new eyes. The city had grown physically, stretching out far to the west, and it had also taken on a new sophistication and vitality. Borges found the cultural life of Buenos Aires as stimulating as that of any city in Europe. As soon as the family settled in a house on Bulnes Street, near their old Palermo neighborhood, Borges plunged into the exciting café circuit of the capital. "I remember that in all the cafés there were intriguing characters who created excitement and interest," he told an interviewer in the 1980s.

The most fascinating character for Borges was Macedonio Fernández, a novelist who had been born in 1847, the same year as Borges's father. Fernández, a tiny man who sported a mustache and a black bowler hat, inspired Borges the same way Rafael Cansinos-

Asséns had inspired him in Spain. He too presided over a literary group that met on Saturday nights. Borges went through the week impatiently, waiting for the moment when he could hear what Fernández would come up with. As Borges recalled, Fernández would only open his mouth three or four times in an evening—but everything he said was striking and original.

Fernández was apparently even more offbeat than Cansinos. Borges reports that among other things, he went to bed with all his clothes on, wrapping a towel around his head to ward off drafts. According to Borges's reminiscence, Fernández also delighted in confusing his friends:

> Macedonio was fond of compiling small oral catalogs of people of genius, and in one of them I was amazed to find a very lovable lady of our acquaintance, Quica González Acha de Tomkinson Alvear. I stared at him open-mouthed. I somehow did not think Quica ranked with Hume and Schopenhauer [two of Borges's and Fernández's favorite philosophers]. But Macedonio said, "Philosophers have had to try and explain the universe, while Quica simply feels and understands it." He would turn to her and ask, "Quica, what is Being?" Quica would answer, "I don't know what you mean, Macedonio." "You see," he would say to me, "she understands so perfectly that she cannot even grasp the fact that we are puzzled."

If Borges was something of a shut-in during his earliest years, as a young man he became a bundle of energy. He explored the streets of Buenos Aires tirelessly, until there was no part of the city he did not know. At the same time, he plunged into literary activity with a passion, appointing himself the champion of ultraism in Argentina. He and several other young writers published a literary magazine entitled *Prisma* (Prism). In fact, the magazine was published as a single sheet the size of a poster. Each issue contained a statement of the aims of ultraism, a group of poems, and a woodcut by Norah Borges, who was on her way to a successful career as an

Borges in his twenties. Shy and withdrawn during his boyhood, Borges showed a new self-confidence after his years in Europe. While working hard at his poetry, he joined discussion groups and helped found a literary magazine, Prisma.

artist. Each time a new issue was published, Borges and his friends roamed the streets throughout the night, plastering their creations to the walls of Buenos Aires.

Borges's father had always advised him not to rush into print, but by 1923 he was ready to collect his poems into a 64-page book entitled *Fervor de Buenos Aires* (Adoration of Buenos Aires). According to Borges, the book "celebrated sunsets, solitary places, and unfamiliar corners; it ventured into Berkeleyan metaphysics and family history; it recorded early loves." In later years, Borges believed that he had tried to cram too much into this small volume, but he recognized that it contained all the major themes he was to explore in later books.

Borges's father put up the money to cover the printing costs, and 300 copies of *Fervor de Buenos Aires* were produced. Borges had no notion of making money on the book and gave away most of the copies to his friends. Perhaps out of modesty, he found a subtle way of distributing his work:

> Having noticed that many people who went to the offices
> of *Nosotros*—one of the old, more solid literary magazines
> of the time—left their overcoats hanging in the cloak room,
> I brought fifty or a hundred copies to Alfredo Bianchi, one
> of the editors. Bianchi stared at me in amazement and said,
> "Do you expect me to sell these books for you?" "No," I
> answered. "Although I've written them, I'm not altogether
> a lunatic. I thought I might ask you to slip some of these
> books into the pockets of those coats hanging out there."
> He generously did so. When I came back after a year's ab-
> sence, I found that some of the inhabitants of the over-
> coats had read my poems, and a few had even written
> about them. As a matter of fact, in this way I got myself
> a small reputation as a poet.

The year's absence was caused by a second family trip to Europe, arranged so that the elder Borges could see his eye doctor in Geneva. Young Jorge was not eager to leave his literary life in Buenos Aires—or the young woman whose long hair had inspired several of his poems. But his father had been supporting him, and if he stayed behind, he would have had to find a job and thus give up much of the time he devoted to writing.

Upon returning to his old haunts in Spain, Borges found that the ultraist movement was dead. He also discovered that he himself still had admirers in the literary community. He began to publish poems in *Revista de Occidente* (Western Review), edited by the most important thinker in Spain, José Ortega y Gasset. In the same journal, Ramón Gómez de la Serna, one of the leading writers of the day, published a review of *Fervor de Buenos Aires* in which he affectionately recalled Borges's first visit to Spain and praised a number of things in the poems. This was a great honor for a young writer; although in his "Autobiographical Essay" Borges downplayed the reception of his work in Spain, it must have given him a great lift at the time.

Borges returned to Argentina in the middle of 1924. To his dismay, the young woman he had been reluctant to part with had cut her long hair, and she no longer inspired him. On a happier note, the ultraist movement Borges had founded was flourishing in Buenos Aires. The center of activity was a magazine called *Martín Fierro*, named after the 19th-century epic poem by José Hernández that celebrated the deeds of the gauchos, or Argentine cowboys. Borges published a poem and a pair of articles in *Martín Fierro*, but before long he found backing for a magazine of his own, *Prow*. All in all, Borges produced seven books between 1921 and 1930. In later years, he expressed little pride in this body of work, claiming that he spent many years buying up old copies of these youthful books and burning them. Nevertheless, this period of intense activity established Borges as a force in Argentine literature and allowed him to find his identity as a writer.

That identity was not easy to come by. Borges was widely respected as a leader of the new movements in Argentine literature, but he was also seen as something of an oddity, a delicate creature who had been nurtured on foreign literature in a comfortable home. This view of him became evident when the editors of *Martín Fierro* decided, as a publicity stunt, to make up a literary feud between two groups of Argentine writers. They called the two

Actor Rudolph Valentino performs the tango in a 1921 film. Valentino made the tango a respectable dance, but for Borges it was a symbol of the Buenos Aires underworld, where it originated. During the 1920s, Borges spent many hours exploring the city's slums, in search of literary material.

groups Florida and Boedo, after a pair of well-known neighborhoods in Buenos Aires. Florida was a prosperous street filled with theaters, cafés, bookshops, and art galleries; Boedo was a residential working-class quarter. Hence, the Florida writers were the ivory-tower types, and the Boedo writers were closer to the people. Without consulting him, the editors of *Martín Fierro* assigned Borges to the Florida group. When he protested that he really belonged with the Boedos, they told him it was too late to switch. Although Borges later dismissed the entire episode as a "put-up job" and a "sham," it clearly distressed him at the time.

Whether or not his fellow writers were aware of it, Borges was doing everything possible to distance himself from the comfortable world he belonged to by birth. He spent much of his time exploring the Northside, a section of Buenos Aires frequented by underworld characters. He became fascinated with the slang of the area, *lunfardo*, a dialect made up of Italian and Portuguese words, and with the tango, a slow, sensual dance performed by hoodlums, which in a cleaned-up form became popular throughout the world during the 1920s. Borges's model in this pursuit was the poet Evaristo Carriego. Carriego, who died of tuberculosis in 1912, had been a neighbor of the Borgeses and the first Argentine writer to celebrate the culture of the Northside. The young Borges had admired Carriego and set out to follow in his footsteps. In later life, he admitted to an interviewer that his experiences had perhaps been a bit more tame than those of his idol.

> Yes, [Carriego] personally met almost all the criminals
> of his time. I, on the other hand, also met them, but only
> when they were somewhat on the sidelines, when they
> had already retired. I met the *guapo* [tough guy] Nicolás
> Paredes, for example, when he was very old, and I became
> a friend of his. The last time I visited him at his house, he
> gave me a present—an orange. He lived in abject poverty,
> and before I left, he said: "No one leaves my house empty-
> handed, Borges." And as he couldn't find anything else to

give me, he gave me an orange, which I would have liked to preserve forever.

Borges's mother took a dim view of her son's fascination with the Northside, whose residents she considered "a bunch of bums." She also believed that Carriego had been a bad influence on Borges. When Borges wrote a book-length essay on Carriego in 1930, he felt that he had to give his mother some excuse. He pointed out that the dead poet had, after all, been a neighbor. He was wasting his breath. "If you are going to write a book about each of our neighbors," his mother replied, "we are finished."

During this period, Leonor Acevedo de Borges began to emerge as the mainstay of her family. The Borgeses had moved to a sixth-floor apartment with spectacular views of midtown Buenos Aires. They were in comfortable enough circumstances, but Jorge Guillermo Borges was now completely blind and dependent on his wife. Leonor Borges, who had always represented the purely Argentine heritage of the family, now began to perfect her English so that she could read her husband's favorite books to him. There were also signs that she might eventually have to fulfill the same role for her son: In 1927, Borges underwent an operation for cataracts, a condition in which the lens of the eye becomes clouded. The operation was successful, and Borges was able to carry on reading and writing as before. But in the years to come he would need to have seven more operations, in a futile attempt to preserve his sight.

Apart from the difficulty with his eyes, Borges had little to complain of. In 1929, his third collection of poetry and essays, *Cuaderno San Martín* (the brand name of the notebook in which Borges wrote), was awarded the Second Municipal Prize, which carried the substantial award of 3,000 pesos. Borges used part of the money to purchase a secondhand set of the *Encyclopaedia Britannica*, which was eventually to have more influence on his mature writing

An ancient Egyptian labyrinth, as depicted in a 17th-century drawing. The labyrinth, a maze with only one way out and many false turnings, fascinated Borges throughout his life and played an increasingly important role in his writing.

than did his excursions into the slums. The money also gave him more time to write without worrying about earning a living. At the age of 30, Borges had yet to hold a full-time job.

Much of his energy was devoted to forming friendships that were to last throughout his life. ("Friendship is, I think, the one redeeming Argentine passion," he later wrote.) In 1925, he met Victoria Ocampo, an attractive, intelligent, and forceful woman who was nine years older than Borges. Ocampo, who had been brought up by a French governess, had been so steeped in French culture that she wrote her books in French and had them translated into Spanish so that they could be published in Argentina. (In this light, she could certainly sympathize with the deep influence of English language and literature on Borges.) Upon meeting the Borges family, she was immediately charmed by Jorge and Norah, of whom she said, "They both, in their different ways, seemed to walk a few inches above the earth we all tread on." Later on, as editor of *Sur* (The South), perhaps the most influential literary magazine in Latin America, Ocampo was to prove a great champion of Borges's writing.

Another of Borges's great friends was Alejandro Xul-Solar, a poet, painter, and mystic. Xul-Solar, whose real name was Schultz, was a charming eccentric in the vein of Macedonio Fernández and Rafael Cansinos-Asséns. "I remember asking him on one particularly sultry afternoon," Borges recalled, "about what he had done that stifling day. His answer was 'Nothing whatever, except for founding twelve religions after lunch.'" Borges also met a 17 year old named Elsa Astete Millán and took a fancy to her. Millán, however, did not return Borges's admiration and eventually married someone else. According to Emir Rodriguez Monegal, this would not normally have had any lasting effect on Borges: "In spite of his reputation as an intellectual and a bookworm, Georgie was terribly susceptible to beautiful young women. He was constantly though briefly falling madly in love." This time, however, Borges did not forget the object of his passion. Many years later, when Millán was a widow and Borges a 67-year-old bachelor, he married her.

On the whole, the 1920s were an innocent and joyful time for Borges, filled with experimentation and accomplishment—much the same could be said for the world at large, which was enjoying peace, prosperity, and rapid progress after the nightmare of the

First World War. But new problems were on the horizon in the form of a worldwide economic depression and, eventually, another world war. In Argentina itself, the first sign of change came in 1930, when a military revolt overthrew the government of President Hipólito Irigoyen, ending 14 years of democracy and ushering in the "infamous decade" of the 1930s.

Hipólito Irigoyen (right), known as the Mole, served two terms as president of Argentina during the 1910s and 1920s. Borges both supported and criticized Irigoyen at different times, but he preferred the Mole to the military men who overthrew him.

CHAPTER FIVE

The Infamous Decade

In 1853, following the overthrow of the brutal dictator General Juan Manuel de Rosas, Argentina adopted a political system based on that of the United States. Under a series of elected presidents, the nation made great economic progress throughout the 19th century, becoming one of the world's leading exporters of beef and grain. But Argentina was unable to achieve the same political stability enjoyed by its North American counterpart. The upper classes controlled the government and showed little concern with the plight of the poor; officials took graft and rigged elections; and presidents usually picked their successors in order to ensure conservative rule. However, the adoption of the secret ballot in 1912 made it possible for Argentines to hold honest elections, and in 1916 the people chose Hipólito Irigoyen as president.

Irigoyen, known as the Mole because of his reluctance to appear in public, concentrated on social reforms and education during his first term as president (1916–22) and enjoyed wide public support. Borges, though never deeply interested in politics, nevertheless found Irigoyen an appealing figure. In an article written in 1925—when Irigoyen, even though retired, was still running the government from behind the scenes—Borges compared him favorably to Rosas, the 19th-century dictator. Although Borges recognized that both men shared a tendency to trample on their opponents, he admired them for capturing the devotion of the people and for conducting themselves in a restrained style. This was a curious point of view for Borges, whose ancestors had shed their blood to rid the country of Rosas. Borges's biographer Emir Rodriguez Monegal suggests that it may have been a declaration of independence from his family, on whom he still relied for the necessities of life. In other words, Borges was assuming a pose rather than taking a stand.

Monegal's idea gains credence from the way Borges reacted when Irigoyen tried to regain the presidency in 1928. Although Borges spearheaded the Committee of Young Intellectuals to back the former president, he made it clear that he was doing so because he felt that Irigoyen's enemies would tamper with the votes and cause his defeat. It would be both noble and romantic to stand up for a lost cause. When Irigoyen surprised everyone by getting elected after all, Borges began to criticize the regime harshly. As it turned out, Irigoyen, nearing the age of 80, was unable to cope with the problems facing the nation. When the military supplanted him, Borges's reaction showed that he was, in the end, completely fed up with politics: "Before . . . we had stupidity but with it the noisy opposition newspapers, the 'Long Live' and 'Death To' which flourished on the walls, in tangos and milongas; now we have *Independence Under Martial Law*, a fawning press, . . . and the established myth that the former regime was cruel and tyrannical."

With one repressive government following another, the 1930s proved to be tortuous years for Argentina. They were, however, years of achievement for Borges. In 1932, he published a fourth collection of essays, *Discusión* (Discussion). The book is especially noteworthy because it marked Borges's first appearance in print as a film critic. He had been devoted to movies since the growth of silent films during the early 20th century and had spent many afternoons in darkened theaters, perhaps at some cost to his fragile eyesight, watching the flickering images on the silver screen. As a critic, Borges proved to be a keen judge of talent. He was among the first to appreciate the genius of Charlie Chaplin, the king of silent-film comedy. In later years he championed the work of the American actor and director Orson Welles, particularly *Citizen Kane*, released in 1941 and considered by many to be the greatest of all American films. Even after he went blind during the 1950s, Borges continued to attend the movies, listening to the dialogue while a friend gave him occasional clues as to what was taking place on the screen. He also collaborated on screenplays with Adolfo Bioy Casares, an Argentine writer to whom he was introduced by Victoria Ocampo when Borges was 30 and Bioy Casares was only 17 but already a published author.

Orson Welles, the actor and film director, on the set of his 1941 classic, Citizen Kane. *Borges, an avid moviegoer and a serious film critic, was among the first to appreciate Welles's unusual gifts.*

Borges's growing importance as a writer was confirmed by a roundtable discussion of his work in the magazine *Megáfono* (Megaphone) in August 1933. Most of the participants were Borges's age or younger, and their reactions tended to be typically passionate: They either loved Borges's writing or detested it. One of the older panelists, the Spanish critic Amado Alonso, took a more balanced view. Alonso appreciated Borges's intelligence and sense of humor and understood that he had progressed from a writer who simply wanted to create effects to a writer deeply concerned with describing reality, as he saw it, in precise language. His final judgment was "Borges is worth the trip."

As he was achieving this recognition, Borges was committing himself to the form that would ultimately bring him worldwide fame—the short story. Considering the briefness of many of his best stories, many readers might conclude that he found them easy to write. But according to Borges's own testimony, the need for clarity in short stories, the necessity that they have a definite beginning, middle, and end, made him fear at first that he was not up to the task. He was only inspired to attempt his first true short story, "Streetcorner Man," by the death of Nicolás Paredes, the aged brawler who had so proudly given Borges an orange some years before. "I wanted to record something of his voice, his anecdotes, and his particular way of telling them," Borges later wrote. "I slaved over my every page, sounding out each sentence and striving to phrase it in his exact tones." Knowing from experience that his mother disapproved of his writing about people she had called "a bunch of bums," Borges wrote the story in secret over a period of several months.

"Streetcorner Man" was published in the literary section of a rather low grade daily newspaper called *Crítica*, of which Borges was the literary editor. Borges was so unsure of himself that he used a pen name—Francisco Bustos, the name of one of his great-great-grandfathers. As it turned out, the story became so popular that Borges was almost embarrassed by it. The popularity is easy to understand. In racy, vivid language, the story relates an incident in the Villa Santa Rita district of Buenos Aires. The scene is Julia's dance hall, where the local toughs get together to drink rum and dance the tango far into the night. On the night in question, the party is disrupted by a group from the Northside. Their champion, the Butcher, is seeking a knife fight with Rosendo Juárez, the local hero: "Everyone knew that [Rosendo] had at least a couple of killings to his credit. He usually wore a soft hat with a narrow brim and tall crown, and it would sit in a cocky way on his long hair, which he slicked straight back. Lady luck smiled on him, as they say, and around Villa all of us who were younger used to ape him—even as to how he spit."

But on this particular night, as the narrator (a young tough) tells it, Rosendo disappoints his admirers. Challenged openly by the Butcher, he takes the knife handed to him by La Lujanera, his girlfriend—"One look at her could cause a man to lose sleep"—and tosses it out the back window into the river. La Lujanera, disgusted by Rosendo's refusal to fight, goes off with the Butcher, and Rosendo vanishes forever. The narrator describes the way he himself wandered around in the dark, infuriated by the cowardice of the man he had so admired and by the Butcher's unanswered insult to the honor of the whole neighborhood.

> I remained there looking at the things I'd seen all my life—
> the wide sky, the river flowing on blindly, a horse half
> asleep, the dirt roads, the kilns—and I began to realize that,
> in the middle of the ragweed and the dump heaps and that
> whole forsaken neighborhood, I had sprouted up no more
> than a weed myself. With our big mouths and no guts, what
> else would grow there but trash like us? Then I thought
> no, that the worse the place the tougher it has to be.

After a while, the narrator goes back to Julia's, where the dancing has resumed. Before long, the door opens; La Lujanera walks in, and after her comes the Butcher, his chest cut open. As the Butcher

This illustration shows Sheriff Pat Garrett hustling Billy the Kid and his gang off to jail, an event that took place in New Mexico in 1881. In his first book of stories, A Universal History of Infamy, *Borges described the exploits of Billy the Kid and other notorious criminals.*

bleeds to death on the dance floor, La Lujanera describes how someone followed them into a field, challenged the Butcher to a fight, and stabbed him. It was so dark she could not see who it was. Suddenly, someone hears the police coming. Not wanting trouble, the dancers quickly strip the Butcher's corpse of money and jewelry and heave him out the window into the river. The narrator goes home, and the last sentence of the story reveals what the reader has previously only been able to guess: "I turned the blade over, slowly. It was as good as new, innocent-looking, and there wasn't the slightest trace of blood on it."

"Streetcorner Man," despite its success, was not the type of writing Borges wanted to pursue. He may well have been afraid of becoming a popular writer of stories on the daily life of Buenos Aires; this kind of popularity, however enjoyable, would have made it difficult for Borges to explore the more complicated ideas that had always interested him. He had no intention of writing a sequel to "Streetcorner Man." But he could never, throughout his life, shake his fascination with the story's main themes—honor, courage, cowardice, the code of the duel. In the summer of 1934, while visiting his cousin Esther Haedo at her ranch along the Brazil-Uruguay border, Borges found the impetus to continue his story writing. As he later told Professor Willis Barnstone:

> I was rather bored, but I saw a man killed. I had never seen that before. He was an old Uruguayan herd drover. He was killed by a Negro with a revolver, who got two shots into him, and he died. And I thought, what a pity. And then I thought no more about it. But afterwards, in the many years that came after those ten days . . . the place came back to me, and I seem to be always recalling it. It is very strange. I have traveled more or less all over the world. I have seen great cities. . . . Yet I don't know why my mind goes back to that shabby little town on the Brazilian border and, when I am writing, it seems to inspire me. And yet, at the time, it was not especially interesting. The whole thing happened in memory afterwards.

The first result of Borges's strangely delayed inspiration was a volume entitled *A Universal History of Infamy*, which marked the true beginning of his career as a writer of stories. At first glance, the stories might be considered a continuation of "Streetcorner Man" because most of them chronicle the lives of infamous outlaws, including Billy the Kid, the vicious gunfighter of the wild West; Monk Eastman, an early-20th-century New York gangster; and the Widow Ching, an 18th-century Chinese pirate. But at the very beginning of the first story, "The Dread Redeemer Lazarus Morell," Borges frees his imagination from the bare facts and lets it roam across centuries and continents: "The Mississippi is a broad-bosomed river, an immense, dim brother of the Paraná, the Uruguay, the Amazon, and the Orinoco. It is a river of muddy waters; each year, disgorged by it, over four hundred million tons of silt profane the Gulf of Mexico. From time immemorial, so much muck has built up a delta where gigantic swamp cypresses grow out of the debris of a continent in perpetual dissolution, and where labyrinths of mud and rushes and dead fish extend the bounds and the peace of this foul-smelling alluvial domain." In story after story, Borges weaves fact and fantasy to create a backdrop against which every human gesture appears both greater and simpler than it would in the everyday world. Reading *A Universal History of Infamy*, it is easy to understand why later Latin American writers such as Fuentes, Cortázar, and García Márquez, praised for their mastery of the technique known as magic realism, felt that they had learned their craft from Borges.

At the time, however, Borges did not consider himself the creator of a new trend in literature or the master of a future generation of novelists. He was mainly concerned with making a living. His newspaper jobs provided a scanty income, and he realized that he had reached an age at which he should be helping his parents rather than the other way around. With a worldwide economic depression in progress, the mid-1930s were not the best time to be looking for work. After talking to a number of friends, Borges

An illustration for Dante's Divine Comedy. *Dante's epic poem, an imaginary trip through hell, purgatory, and heaven, was a constant inspiration to Borges. He later called Dante's work "the greatest gift that literature can give us."*

found a $70-a-month job in a branch of the municipal library. The branch, known as the Miguel Cané, was located in a drab neighborhood in southwestern Buenos Aires. From Borges's description, it is reasonable to guess that most of his fellow employees were neither trained librarians nor genuine lovers of books (as Borges obviously was) but rather a collection of people who had been lucky enough to get on the city payroll:

> There were some fifty of us doing what fifteen could easily have done. My particular job, shared with fifteen or twenty colleagues, was classifying and cataloging the library's holdings, which until that time were uncataloged. The collection, however, was so small that we knew where to find the books without the system, so the system, though laboriously carried out, was never needed or used. The first day, I worked honestly. On the next, some of my fellows took me aside to say that I couldn't do this sort of thing because it showed them up. "Besides," they argued, "as this cataloging has been planned to give us some semblance of work, you'll put us out of our jobs."

Borges adjusted to the system and consoled himself by reading the three volumes of Dante's *Divine Comedy* during the long tram ride back and forth to work. Dante's epic poem, written in Italian during the early 14th century, describes the poet's imaginary journey through hell, purgatory, and heaven. As Borges later told a lecture audience in Buenos Aires, this was just the sort of reading to further define his own purposes as a writer: "A contemporary novel requires five or six hundred pages to make us know somebody, if it ever does. For Dante a single moment is enough. In that moment a person is defined forever. . . . I have wanted to do the same in many stories, and I have been admired for a discovery which actually belongs to Dante in the Middle Ages: that of presenting a moment as a cipher of a life."

Once he reached work, Borges found that he could finish off his duties in an hour and then go down to the basement to con-

The British novelist and essayist Virginia Woolf, photographed during the early 1930s. Now recognized as one of the 20th century's great writers, Woolf was unknown in Latin America until Borges translated her work into Spanish. He undertook the task to fill his idle hours at the Miguel Cané Library.

tinue his reading. On his days off, he pursued his interest in English literature by translating works by the British author Virginia Woolf and the American novelist William Faulkner. These writers, later recognized as among the greatest of the 20th century, were unknown in Latin America during the 1930s, and Borges deserves the credit for introducing them to Spanish-speaking readers.

Borges's co-workers and superiors were completely ignorant of his literary standing, but they were pleased enough with his work to award him a minor promotion. His satisfaction in raising his income was canceled, however, by the death of his father in February 1938. In his "Autobiographical Essay," Borges describes the event in a single sentence: "He had undergone a long agony and was very impatient for his death." As so often happens with Borges, the sentence contains a great deal. It recaptures the character of the father—his endurance, the clarity of his mind up to the last moment—and also the son's awareness of how much he was losing. He was, in fact, being left to carry on without the force that had shaped his mind and given him the courage to pursue his vocation as a writer. It is not surprising that later in the year, on Christmas Eve, he entered upon a mental and physical crisis that reshaped the course of his career.

Juan Perón, president of Argentina from 1946 to 1955, rides in a motorcade with his wife, Eva, in 1952. Borges paid a heavy price for speaking out against Perón's regime: He lost his job and was even threatened with death.

CHAPTER SIX

Teller of Tales

In keeping with the air of mystery that often surrounds Borges, there is no clear record of what happened on Christmas Eve, 1938. According to Borges's own account, he was running up a stairway and felt something graze his scalp: "I had brushed a freshly painted casement window." How this would result in a dangerous cut is unclear. In the story "The South," Borges provides a fictionalized but more vivid description of the accident: "In the obscurity, something brushed by his forehead: a bat, a bird? On the face of the woman who opened the door to him he saw horror engraved, and the hand he wiped across his face came away red with blood." Apparently, a section of the window had swung back into the stairwell, and Borges ran right into it, breaking the glass with his head. A doctor stitched up the cut, which may have been contaminated by chemicals in the wet paint, but failed to disinfect it properly. Borges contracted septicemia, an infection of the bloodstream. After suffering for a week at home, he was rushed to the hospital for an emergency operation, followed by a slow, agonizing recovery. He described the experience in "The South," a story he considered as perhaps his best.

> Fever wasted him and the pictures in *The Thousand and One Nights* served to illustrate nightmares. Friends and relatives paid him visits and, with exaggerated smiles, assured him that they thought he looked fine. Dahlmann listened to them with a kind of feeble stupor and he marveled at their not knowing that he was in hell. A week, eight days passed, and they were like eight centuries. . . . He awoke [in the hospital] with a feeling of nausea, covered with a bandage, in a cell with something of a well about it; in the days and nights which followed the operation he came to realize that he had merely been, up to then, in a suburb of hell. Ice in his mouth did not leave the least trace of freshness. During these days Dahlmann hated himself in minute detail: he hated his identity, his bodily necessities, his humiliation, the beard which bristled upon his face. He stoically endured the curative measures, which were painful, but when the surgeon told him he had been on the point of death from septicemia, Dahlmann dissolved in tears of self-pity for his fate.

In the story, Dahlmann is sent to a ranch in the south—gaucho country—in order to recuperate. Upon arriving, he stops for a meal in a general store. Some local toughs, half-drunk on wine, decide to insult him, and he feels compelled to answer back. Before he knows it, Dahlmann has been given a knife and has accepted a challenge to fight, even though he knows he has little chance. "As he crossed the threshold, he felt that to die in a knife fight, under the open sky, and going forward to the attack, would have been a liberation, a joy, and a festive occasion, on his first night in the sanitorium, when they stuck him with the needle. He felt that if he had been able to choose, then, or to dream his death, this would have been the death he would have chosen or dreamt."

In the story, there are clear echoes of Borges's experiences at his first school, when he submitted to beatings rather than back away from a fight. However, the ending of "The South" is far more romantic, and perhaps less frightening, than the reality of Borges's recovery after being released from the hospital. He knew that he would eventually recover his physical strength, but he feared that his illness had destroyed his mental powers. When his mother offered to read to him, he put her off, terrified that he would not understand the words. When she finally read him a page or two and he found that he did understand, he began to weep with joy.

The next question was, Could he still write? He was afraid to try something easy, such as a review, because if he failed he would know that he was a hopeless case. He decided to try something completely new; if he failed at that, there would always be hope that he could

A 19th-century illustration for Don Quixote *shows Cervantes's knight in his library, surrounded by the imaginary beings that populate his favorite books. Borges's 1938 story about a French author who tries to re-create* Don Quixote *began a new phase in his career.*

still do simpler things. The result of this experiment was "Pierre Menard, Author of *Don Quixote*," a story that many fans of Borges's would choose as perhaps the most typical—if not the best—example of his mature work.

"Pierre Menard" is a brilliant mental exercise in which Borges invents Menard, a French writer, as well as a whole catalog of his writings. According to the narrator, a supposed friend of Menard's, the author's greatest achievement was not his visible work but his *invisible* work. This consisted of the word-for-word reproduction of several portions of *Don Quixote*, the great 17th-century Spanish novel by Miguel de Cervantes. According to the narrator, Menard achieved this feat not by copying from the book but by imagining that he was Cervantes. After quoting two identical passages—one from Menard and one from Cervantes—the narrator decides that they are in fact quite different. For Cervantes, a 17th-century man, to call history "the mother of truth" is quite natural; for Menard to write this more than two centuries later, when philosophers believed that historical events are subject to different interpretations, is truly astonishing. But Menard has really done a great thing; by exposing himself to criticism, he has allowed the reader to approach *Don Quixote* with new eyes. If other writers followed this example, all of literature could be revitalized.

"Pierre Menard," simple in language but complicated in thought, serious and funny at the same time, was a breakthrough on many levels. Among other things, it suggested that reading is as much of an art as is writing—an idea that was to have a powerful influence on literary criticism during the 1970s and 1980s. But the story did not entirely satisfy Borges. He called it a "halfway house between the essay and the true tale," and as he went on, he allowed himself a wider range. After returning to work in the library, he wrote an extraordinary piece entitled "The Library of Babel," in which the universe is described as an endless series of hexagonal, or six-sided, galleries containing an endless number of books that no one can understand.

When it was proclaimed that the Library comprised all books, the first impression was one of extravagant joy. All men felt themselves lords of a secret, intact treasure. There was no personal or universal problem whose eloquent solution did not exist—in some hexagon. The universe was justified, the universe suddenly expanded to the limitless dimensions of hope. . . . Thousands of covetous persons abandoned their dear natal hexagons and crowded up the stairs, urged on by the vain aim of finding their Vindication. These pilgrims disputed in the narrow corridors, hurled dark maledictions, strangled each other on the divine stairways, flung the deceitful books to the bottom of the tunnels, and died as they were thrown into space by men from remote regions. Some went mad. . . .

The Vindications do exist. I have myself seen two of these books, which were concerned with future people, people who were perhaps not imaginary. But the searchers did not remember that the calculable possibility of a man's finding his own book, or some perfidious variation of his own book, is next to zero.

In other words, the universe is another labyrinth, a series of endless reflecting mirrors, in which we continually lose our way. This is the theme that Borges went on to explore, mixing humor, philosophy, and drama, in story after story. In "The Circular Ruins," for example, he tells the story of a wizard who, night after night over a period of years, creates a living man in his dreams. At the end of his labors, he submits to the fire that surrounds the ruins of the temple where he has had his dreams: "He walked towards the sheets of flame. They did not bite his flesh, they caressed him and flooded him without heat or combustion. With relief, with humiliation, with terror, he understood that he also was an illusion, that someone else was dreaming him." The reader is left to understand that whoever is dreaming of the wizard is himself being dreamed of by a third person, and the third person by a fourth, and so on.

An astrologer's den, as depicted in an 18th-century engraving, features a chart of the heavens (on table) and a globe (at left) decorated with the signs of the zodiac. Mystical symbols and writings intrigued Borges, and he used them freely in such stories as "Death and the Compass."

Although Borges now rarely wrote a story that lacked a philosophical framework, he did not lose the storytelling gifts that had marked his earlier tales of violence and adventure. "Death and the Compass," for example, is an intriguing mystery story in which a detective discovers that a series of three murders corresponds to the tetragrammaton, the letters representing the name of God in sacred Jewish writings. By tracing the pattern on a map, he is able to predict where the fourth murder will occur, although, to the surprise of the reader, he is unable to prevent it. In "The Garden of the Forking Paths," a learned and mysterious Chinese spy, employed by the Germans during World War I, uses an unwitting English scholar—who has solved a labyrinth devised by one of the spy's ancestors—to accomplish his mission. Borges was thrilled when *Mystery Magazine*, published in the United States, awarded him a prize for "The Garden of the Forking Paths." "I felt proud," he recalled, "above all that they would take me seriously, a mere writer from the Río de la Plata."

When discussing his career, Borges was often guilty of excessive modesty. But the truth is that even as he began to produce his best work during the 1940s, he was not well known outside a small group of Argentine writers and intellectuals who enthusiastically read his stories and articles in various Buenos Aires newspapers and magazines. His co-workers at the library were unaware of his literary reputation; when one of them found an entry for the writer Jorge Luis Borges in a reference book, he was amazed that this man had both the same name and the same birthdate as the Borges who worked at the library.

Borges the citizen, on the other hand, was compelled to be highly visible. Throughout the 1930s, political conditions both in Argentina and throughout the world grew progressively more dangerous. In Europe, economic depression and the fear of a workers' revolution contributed to the rise of Fascist regimes in Italy and Germany. Benito Mussolini had become the ruler of Italy in 1926; in Germany, Adolf Hitler and his Nazi party had taken over the government in 1933. Both men indulged themselves in dreams of

Fascist dictators Adolf Hitler of Germany (left) and Benito Mussolini of Italy confer in 1935. Hitler and Mussolini had many supporters in Argentina, but Borges was one of their fiercest opponents. In his magazine articles, he condemned and ridiculed Fascist myths of racial superiority.

national glory, despised democracy, and crushed their opponents with ruthless brutality. Due to the violent nature of Argentine politics and the large number of Italian immigrants in the country, Mussolini in particular had a large following in Argentina. There were also many German sympathizers in the army, which had been trained by German officers in past years. The situation was further complicated in 1936, when a civil war broke out in Spain, pitting the army and the Catholic church against the liberal government and its left-wing supporters. Many of the Spanish immigrants to Argentina were conservative and religious, and they strongly supported the rebellion led by General Francisco Franco.

Argentina's writers and artists were forced to take sides on the issues that were driving the world toward another catastrophic war. Many of Borges's friends, such as Victoria Ocampo, proclaimed their opposition to fascism. Borges himself, after his ill-fated support of President Irigoyen in 1928, had tried to avoid political meetings and public manifestos. However, in the articles and reviews he published in the magazine *El Hogar* (The Home), he expressed his disgust with the anti-Jewish campaign being waged by the German Nazis—a campaign that would eventually result in concentration camps and mass extermination. He was especially scornful of the books being published in Germany, both those that portrayed Jews in a negative light and those that showed the "true" German as tall, muscular, blond, and blue eyed.

When some Argentine Fascists suggested that Borges himself was Jewish, he responded with a humorous article entitled "I, a Jew." Unlike his old friend Rafael Cansinos-Asséns, however, he did not actually proclaim himself a Jew but rather—which was perhaps Cansinos's real intent—proceeded to make fun of the people who took such questions seriously. Borges began the article by admitting that a certain Argentine historian had once identified Acevedo, Borges's mother's name, as being of Portuguese-Jewish origin. However, he claimed, his own family had carefully investigated the subject and found no Jewish roots. Borges sadly concluded that he might never know the truth about his ancestry. But he wondered aloud why people were always hunting for descendants of one ancient people and not the others: "Our inquisitors are seeking Hebrews, never Phoenicians, Numidians, Scythians, Babylonians, Huns, Vandals, Ostrogoths, Ethiopians, Illyrians, Paphlagonians, Sarmatians, Medes, Ottomans, Berbers, Britons, Lybians, Cyclops, and Lapiths. The nights of Alexandria, Babylon, Carthage, and Memphis have never succeeded in engendering one single grandfather; only the tribes of the bituminous Black Sea had that power."

When World War II broke out in September 1939, Borges made it clear that his sympathies were with Britain and France in their struggle with the Fascist powers Germany and Italy. A good portion of the Argentine people felt the same way, but the army was increasingly pro-Fascist. In 1943, deciding that Argentina's civilian government was becoming too pro-British, the army took control of the country. The military men clamped down on the press and the labor movement and arrested leading members of opposition parties.

By 1945, even though the victory of the Allies in Europe was assured, fascism still reigned in Argentina. The leading member of the Argentine government was Colonel Juan Domingo Perón, who continued to repress all opposition while cleverly introducing social reforms to increase his popularity.

The government had allowed Borges to continue at the Miguel Cané Library throughout the war. But when Perón was elected president in 1946—despite his Fascist beliefs and his brutality, his reforms won him wide support among the Argentine workers—Borges found himself a marked man. Before long, he was informed that he had been "promoted" from the library to the post of inspector of chickens and rabbits in a public market. This was a calculated insult for a writer of his stature, and Borges immediately resigned his new post, leaving himself completely unemployed. His friends and admirers quickly organized a banquet for him, at which his public response to Perón was read: "Dictatorships foment sub-

A pro-Perón demonstration in Buenos Aires, 1955. (The banner reads, "We Want Perón.") During the Perón years, the political and cultural atmosphere of Buenos Aires disgusted Borges. "He was like a man skinned alive," a friend recalled.

servience, dictatorships foment cruelty; even more abominable is the fact that they foment stupidity. . . . To fight against those sad monotonies is one of the many duties of writers."

Borges, who had tried so hard to stay out of politics, now found himself the symbol of resistance to Perón. Fortunately, he was able to make a living by teaching English literature and lecturing on an astonishing variety of subjects—poetry, philosophy, religion, Chinese and Persian thought, Jewish mysticism. Borges, who had always been shy and tended to stammer when speaking in public, was at first sick with fear about giving lectures. But once he began his series of talks, he found that he enjoyed it. "I went from town to town," he recalled, "staying overnight in hotels I'd never see again. Sometimes my mother or a friend accompanied me. Not only did I end up making far more money than at the library but I enjoyed the work and felt that it justified me."

Emir Rodriguez Monegal, who knew Borges well during this period, recalled that the reality was more difficult than Borges's happy memory. He approached each lecture with painstaking care, taking pages of notes and rehearsing until he knew the entire lecture by heart. Monegal is careful to point out that all this took place "in the context of Perón's Argentina. . . . Buenos Aires was then literally wallpapered with enormous posters of Perón and his blonde wife, and each poster was covered with aggressive slogans." Borges continued to walk the streets with his friends, but the city he had rediscovered in 1921 and had come to love no longer existed. It must have galled him to see the walls on which he had once put up posters filled with poetry and art now covered by vulgar tributes to a brutal dictator. "While he walked," Monegal remembered, "Borges' pain was visible in the bitterness of his speech and the brusqueness of his gestures, rather than in the actual words he used. He was like a man skinned alive."

The Perón regime was not always content to let Borges suffer in this private manner. In September 1948, for example, Borges's mother and sister were arrested for taking part in a political protest in downtown Buenos Aires. The women involved were all sentenced to a month in prison. Because of her advanced age, Leonor Borges was allowed to serve her sentence by staying in the house for a month, with a police guard at the door. But Norah, who now had a family of her own, was put into a jail usually reserved for prostitutes, a move designed to humiliate her and break her spirit. The police told Norah that if she wrote a letter of apology to the dictator's wife, Eva Perón—a former radio performer who might

Juan Perón (center) visits the offices of La Prensa, *Argentina's leading newspaper, which his government took over in order to stifle dissent. Borges detested not only Perón's policies but also the dictator's thirst for personal glory, evidenced by the huge portraits of him and his wife.*

have stepped out of an early Borges story—she would be set free. Norah preferred to remain in jail. With typical spirit, she even transformed her ordeal into a positive experience, drawing pictures of the jail and the other inmates, whom she portrayed as angels.

Borges later recalled the courage his mother showed when the government sent someone to threaten the family even more directly:

> The fellow came late at night, and my mother answered the door. "I am going to kill you and your son," said a voice, appropriately harsh and professionally malevolent. "Why?" asked my mother. "Because I am a Peronist," added the unknown man. Then my mother answered him: "Well, if you want to kill my son, it's very easy. He leaves home for his office every morning at eight; all you have to do is wait for him. As for myself, señor, I have turned eighty, and I advise you to hurry up if you want to kill me, because I might very well die on you beforehand."

The Borgeses were never bothered by this shady visitor again, although a police agent often followed Borges around and took notes at his lectures. (Borges eventually got to know this man, and the agent admitted that he too detested Perón but wanted to keep his job.) Through it all, Borges continued to write. One of his best-known stories, "The Aleph," dates from this period and could be taken as a good summation of Borges's way of coping with the misery around him. In the story, a narrator named Borges describes his relationship with an arrogant, second-rate poet named Carlos Argentino Daneri. Borges was in love with Carlos Argentino's cousin Beatriz, who has recently died, and he visits the poet to keep in touch with her memory. Both Carlos Argentino and his poetry depress the Borges of the story, much the way Argentina itself (and the cherished things that had died in it) depressed Borges the author. The poet, however, needs to confide in Borges.

The owners of his house want to tear it down to put up a fancy shop, and he is trying to fight them in court. He must keep the house, he explains, because on the cellar stairs there is an Aleph, the point at which all points converge and everything is revealed. Without the knowledge that he draws from the Aleph, Carlos Argentino will not be able to finish the great poem he is working on. He convinces Borges to lie on the cellar floor in the dark and watch the stairs. Borges agrees, and just as Carlos Argentino predicted, there is the Aleph, a glowing spot in which Borges sees everything that has ever existed, from all the mirrors in the world to the circulation of his own blood. "I felt infinite veneration," the narrator declares, "infinite compassion." But when he goes upstairs, he takes his revenge on Carlos Argentino by acting as though he has seen nothing. Take my advice, he tells the poet, let them tear down the house, spend some time in the country, it will be good for your nerves. After Carlos Argentino has left Buenos Aires, Borges reads some scholarly books and convinces himself that the Aleph in Carlos Argentino's house was not even the real Aleph, which resides in a stone column in a mosque in Egypt: "Did I see it when I saw all things, and have I forgotten it? Our minds are porous with forgetfulness; I myself am falsifying and losing, through the tragic erosion of the years, the features of Beatriz."

"The Aleph" can be understood on many levels, and undoubtedly Borges did not intend it as a political statement. But it is difficult not to see in it a vivid portrait of Borges during the Perón years, surrounded by things he cannot tolerate, yet finding in the midst of it all remarkable visions—and best of all, never giving those he despises the satisfaction of knowing what he thinks and feels. The story is a good illustration of the attitude toward life and politics that Borges expressed to an interviewer in later years: "I think I am physically a coward, but not mentally. I have never pandered to power or to the mob. I think that I am a brave man in the serious sense of the word."

Borges speaking to an audience in Madrid, Spain, in 1963. After winning the International Publishers Prize in 1961, Borges began to travel for the first time since the 1920s. During his 1963 visit to Europe, he was reunited with many of his old friends.

CHAPTER SEVEN

800,000 Books and Darkness

By 1955, Argentina had had enough of Juan Perón. In September, the army and navy rose up in revolt, and Perón had no choice but to resign and flee the country. In his "Autobiographical Essay," Borges recalled the joyous occasion:

> After a sleepless, anxious night, nearly the whole population [of Buenos Aires] came out into the streets, cheering the revolution and shouting the name of Córdoba, where most of the fighting had taken place. We were so carried away that for some time we were quite unaware of the rain that was soaking us to the bone. We were so happy that not a single word was even uttered against the fallen dictator.

Argentina's new rulers were also military men, but they were anxious to show the world that they were not about to follow in the footsteps of Perón. One of their major concerns was to revitalize the cultural life of the nation. In accordance with this policy, they named Borges director of the National Library.

Borges himself could have wished for nothing better than this appointment, which erased all his humiliations during the previous decade. He cherished the memory of visiting the library with his father, noting that it was located in the only part of Buenos Aires that had remained unchanged since the days of his childhood. Whereas the elder Borges used to request books on philosophy, young Georgie, too timid to approach the librarians, would simply look through the encyclopedia. Now the books were, in a sense, all his. There was only one thing to temper his joy: Borges could no longer read the books. He was blind.

In keeping with his subtle approach to the world, Borges referred to his affliction as a "modest" blindness. He pointed out, in a 1977 lecture, that he was only completely blind in one eye. With the other, he perceived a bluish green mist and was able to distinguish the color yellow, "the color of the tiger." He lamented the loss

Although Borges was completely blind in one eye, he could still make out certain colors with the other. To his delight, he could still see yellow, "the color of the tiger," an animal he had loved ever since his childhood visits to the zoo.

of the color red—"that color which shines in poetry, and which has so many beautiful names in many languages"—but otherwise took a wry and philosophical view of his situation. He noted that two of the library's previous directors, José Mármol and Paul Groussac, had also been blind, and he felt that there was a certain destiny in the number 3: "I speak of God's splendid irony in granting me at one time 800,000 books and darkness."

Despite his blindness, Borges tackled his new job with enthusiasm. He was determined to make the library a center of culture again, just as it had been during his youth, when Groussac was director. He made plans to reissue the library's official journal and also organized a series of lectures. Emir Rodriguez Monegal, invited to give one of the lectures, was amazed by Borges's vitality during a tour of the library: "He roams long corridors lined with books; he quickly turns corners and gets into passages which are truly invisible, mere cracks in the walls of books; he rushes down winding staircases which abruptly end in the dark. There is almost no light in the library's corridors and staircases. I try to follow him, tripping, blinder and more handicapped than Borges because my only guides are my eyes. In the dark of the library Borges finds his way with the precarious precision of a tightrope walker."

Borges was determined to make of his blindness a new experience rather than a misfortune. As he later told an interviewer, Roberto Alifano, "A writer—and, I believe, generally all persons—must think that whatever happens to him or her is *a resource*. All things have been given to us for a purpose." One of his first projects was to recapture the English side of his heritage through the study of Anglo-Saxon, the language spoken in England before the Norman conquest in 1066. With the aid of his students at the Association of English Culture, he delved into Anglo-Saxon literature:

> And then we began to read, and we fell in love with two
> words. And those two words were the Saxon words for Lon-
> don and for Rome. London was called Lundenburgh. . . .
> Rome was called, by the Anglo-Saxons, Romaburgh. We fell

Borges in the National Library of Argentina, of which he was appointed director in 1955. Borges tackled the job with great enthusiasm; the library had suffered during the Perón years, and he was determined to make it a force in the cultural life of Argentina.

in love with those two words, and we found a beautiful sentence in the Anglo-Saxon *Chronicle.* It said: Julius Caesar, or Julius the Caesar, was the first Roman to seek out Britain. *Gaius Iulius se Casere ærest Romana Brytenland gesohte.* And then we ran along a street called Perú in Buenos Aires, shouting "Iulius se Casere. . ." And people stared at us. We did not mind. We had found beauty!

As a writer, however, Borges was severely hampered by his blindness. His immediate solution was to return to poetry. He found that he could keep several lines of poetry in his head and refine them mentally without having to see them on paper. When he was ready to set the words down, he could dictate them to an assistant. Borges took courage from the knowledge that two of the

The English poet John Milton (1608–74) was already blind when he wrote his epic poem Paradise Lost. *Milton's example encouraged Borges to return to poetry after losing his own sight. "All things have been given to us for a purpose," said Borges.*

world's greatest poets had been blind—Homer, the ancient Greek, and John Milton, the author of the 17th-century epic *Paradise Lost.* "It is obviously easier to remember verse than prose," he wrote, "and to remember regular verse forms rather than free ones. Regular verse is, so to speak, portable. One can walk down the street or be riding the subway while composing or polishing a sonnet, for rhyme and meter have mnemonic [memory-aiding] virtues."

Fortunately, he also had many people around him eager to help. Borges was now a heroic figure to the young people of Argentina, and he attracted a group of students and followers, mostly women, who were always available to take dictation or read to him. For his everyday activities, he was now completely reliant on his mother, with whom he had lived since 1944 in a pleasant apartment on Maipú Street in downtown Buenos Aires. Leonor Borges was still a vibrant and energetic woman who looked a good 20 years younger than her age—people frequently took her to be Borges's sister rather than his mother. Since the death of her husband, she had emerged more and more as a personality in her own right and had begun to earn money by translating English authors into Spanish. In addition to looking after Borges's basic needs, she was always there to read to him and take dictation. She had, whether she liked it or not, become so immersed in her son's imaginary world that she even gave him the last line of one of his stories, "The Intruder," a rather grisly tale of two brothers who love the same woman and resolve their rivalry by killing her. "Then she asked me not to write any more of those blood-and-thunder stories," Borges recalled. "She was sick and tired of them. But she gave me the words, and at that moment she became, in a sense, one of the characters in the story, and she actually believed in it. She said 'I know what he said' as though the thing had actually occurred."

Borges began to feel that he himself was becoming a character in a Borges story, and he tried to describe this odd sensation in "Borges and I." Accustomed to being known within a fairly tight circle of writers and artists, he now found himself a national figure. Between 1955 and 1960, five books appeared in Argentina on the subject of Borges's work, and two of his stories were turned into films. In 1956, he was granted an honorary doctorate by the University of Cuyo and was appointed professor of English and American literature at the University of Buenos Aires. In the same year, he won the National Prize of Literature. But who was getting all this attention? Was it the Borges who had spent all those years living in Buenos Aires or the Borges who had written the books? Borges the writer was, of course, only one facet of Borges the man—but with his gift for irony, Borges understood that for many people Borges the writer, the pure mental force, was far more real than Borges the man of flesh and blood.

At the time of "Borges and I," however, even Borges the writer was little known outside Latin America. That situation changed dramatically in 1961 when Borges and Samuel Beckett, the Irish novelist and playwright, were jointly awarded the International

Publishers Prize (also known as the Formentor Prize). The prize had been established in 1960 by a group of European and American publishers who specialized in modern literature. The recipients were entitled to a cash award of $10,000, which in this case was split between Beckett and Borges. Emir Rodriguez Monegal points out that Borges did not complain about getting only $5,000: "For an obscure Argentine writer to be cited as one of the indisputable masters of twentieth-century literature was distinction enough. At long last, after a career that covered almost four decades, Borges had the fame he deserved."

Borges gave credit for his sudden fame to Néstor Ibarra and Roger Callois, who had translated some of his stories into French during the 1940s and had thus given European readers the chance to discover Borges. Before then, he claimed, he was "practically invisible." With the award of the International Publishers Prize, Borges was visible everywhere. *Ficciones*, the 1944 collection that included some of his best stories, appeared in six countries and was

Samuel Beckett, the Irish playwright and novelist, already enjoyed a large following when he shared the 1961 International Publishers Prize with Borges. By contrast, Borges was almost unknown outside Latin America; but the prize brought him worldwide recognition as a master of modern literature.

greeted with praise by readers and critics. It was a great moment not only for Borges but for all of Latin America; no previous Latin American writer had ever achieved such worldwide recognition.

Borges's reception in the United States was especially enthusiastic. In September 1961, the University of Texas invited Borges to spend a semester in Austin as a visiting professor. He accepted eagerly and traveled abroad for the first time since the family trip to Geneva in 1923. The trip was a delightful experience for Borges.

> America . . . had taken on such mythic proportions in my mind that I was sincerely amazed to find there such commonplace things as weeds, mud puddles, dirt roads, flies, and stray dogs. Though at times we fell into homesickness, I know now that my mother—who accompanied me—and I grew to love Texas. She, who always loathed football, even rejoiced over *our* victory when the Longhorns defeated the neighboring [Baylor University] Bears.

In 1963, Borges returned to Europe, visiting Spain, France, Great Britain, and Switzerland. In a sense, he was reliving his past. His old hero, Rafael Cansinos-Asséns, was still living in Madrid; in Geneva, he was reunited with his schoolmates Simon Jichlinski and Maurice Abramowicz and resumed the literary discussions they had enjoyed during the dark days of the First World War. Once he began traveling again, he found it difficult to stop. After visiting several countries in Latin America, he returned to the United States in 1967, spending a year at Harvard University as a visiting professor of poetry. Emir Rodriguez Monegal caught up with Borges at a conference in Oklahoma and observed his effect on the students and faculty to whom he spoke: "They were literally spaced out by his words, by the incantatory way in which he delivered them, by his blindness and almost uncanny face. It was difficult for me to reconcile my many images of Borges—all based on an intimacy with his texts and a friendly, relaxed relationship with the man—with this new Borges."

Monegal had a glimpse of yet another Borges in 1971, when Columbia University invited Borges to New York to receive an honorary degree and take part in a conference. At the time, a group of Puerto Rican students were displeased with the university's role as a landlord in the city's disadvantaged neighborhoods. They chose the conference as an opportunity to stage a political protest, and in the course of a heated discussion, one of the students made some brash and insulting remarks to Borges. According to Monegal, Borges "became furious and, banging on the table, challenged the student to settle matters outside. The student must have been barely twenty. Borges (at seventy-two) was frail, holding his cane in trembling hands. But he meant every word of his chivalrous invitation."

Clearly, Borges was as deeply imbued as ever with the code of bravery that had inspired his earliest stories. When he began to produce more stories in collaboration with other writers—principally Norman Thomas di Giovanni, whom he had met during his stay at Harvard, and his old friend Adolfo Bioy Casares—he often returned to what his mother had called his blood-and-thunder style. "The Meeting," written in 1969, is a chilling story of two men who have an argument over cards at a classy Buenos Aires party. They go outside to fight, using a pair of antique knives that their host had preserved in a glass case. Although neither man has ever been in a duel, they fight skillfully until one of them is killed, whereupon the winner bursts into tears and begs for forgiveness. Years later, the narrator tells this story to a retired police captain, who recognizes the knives from their description: They once belonged to two famous knife fighters, long since dead. The narrator is left with a chilling puzzle:

> I began to wonder whether it was Maneco Uriarte who
> killed Duncan or whether in some uncanny way it could
> have been the weapons, not the men, which fought. I still
> remember how Uriarte's hand shook when he first gripped
> his knife, and the same with Duncan, as though the knives

were coming awake after a long sleep in the cabinet. Even after their gauchos were dust, the knives—the knives, not their tools, the men—knew how to fight. And that night they fought well.

Things last longer than people; who knows whether these knives will meet again, who knows whether the story ends here.

In "Pedro Salvadores," also written in 1969, Borges goes back to 1842, the time of the dictator Rosas. Salvadores, a Buenos Aires gentleman, hides in his cellar to escape Rosas's thugs, who come to the house looking for him. He stays in the cellar for nine years, until the overthrow of the dictator. "Flabby, overweight, Salvadores was the color of wax and could not speak above a low voice. He never got back his confiscated lands; I think he died in poverty. . . . As with so many things, the fate of Pedro Salvadores strikes us as a symbol of something we are about to understand, but never quite do."

Adolfo Bioy Casares, a published author at the age of 17, had been a friend and admirer of Borges's since the 1920s. After Borges's blindness took hold, he and Bioy began to collaborate on stories and film scripts.

Borges was still trying to understand Argentina, still hoping that the past could be put to rest. He even wrote a sequel to his first short story, "Streetcorner Man." In the sequel, "Rosendo's Tale," Rosendo Juárez explains why he backed away from the Butcher's challenge that night in Julia's dance hall: "In that big loudmouth I saw myself, the same as in a mirror, and it made me feel ashamed. I wasn't scared; maybe if I'd been scared I'd have fought with him. . . . To make a clean break with that life, I took off for Uruguay, where I found myself work as a teamster. Since coming back to Buenos Aires I've settled around here. San Telmo always was a respectable neighborhood."

As it turned out, Argentina's agony was not yet over. Nor were the challenges Borges had to face in his search for meaning and final peace.

Borges receives an honorary degree from the University of Puerto Rico in 1981. After achieving his long-awaited recognition in 1961, Borges garnered many additional honors and lectured at universities throughout the world.

CHAPTER EIGHT

The Master

On July 8, 1975, Leonor Acevedo de Borges died at the age of 99. Upon reaching the age of 95, she had complained to her son, "Goodness me, Georgie, I think I overdid it." After that, she had prayed every night not to wake up in the morning. Now she was free, and Borges was on his own.

Borges was to carry on in the apartment under the care of a maid, but this was not the first time he had to get along without his mother's company. In 1967, he married Elsa Astete Millán, whom he had unsuccessfully pursued back in 1927. Her husband had died in 1964, and Borges found that he still admired her after 40 years of separation. Leonor Borges was not in favor of the match. Previously, she had discouraged Borges from getting too close to another woman, María Esther Vázquez, who helped him with his writing and often traveled with him when his mother did not feel up to it. Leonor Borges felt that Vázquez was too young for her son, that he needed an older woman who would be more patient about looking after him in his old age, which was rapidly approaching.

Millán was more suitable in that respect—she was 57 to Borges's 67—but Leonor did not consider her suitable either. Borges had apparently resented his mother's interference with his friendship for Vázquez, and this time he decided to follow his own inclinations.

Borges and his new wife rented a comfortable apartment near the National Library, and for a time everything went smoothly. Borges's mother eventually accepted the marriage, and he continued to visit her regularly. But in 1970, Borges and Millán filed for divorce. Neither of them chose to discuss their differences, but friends, such as Emir Rodriguez Monegal, believed that Millán's inability to speak English was a major problem. Borges's English was not merely flawless; because he had grown up speaking the language and had also studied it with the diligence of a foreigner, many of those he met on his trips to England and the United States felt that he knew English even better than they did. Millán, on the other hand, was unable to share Borges's passion for English and was completely out of her element during visits to English-speaking countries. A lively person who was keenly interested in the world around her, she must have found it very difficult to be left out when Borges conversed for long hours with his British and American friends. In more general terms, Millán and Borges had also lived very different lives. She had grown accustomed to the give-and-take of married life, whereas Borges had never really had to accommodate himself to living with another person as an equal partner.

According to Monegal, Borges later revealed that he had been dismayed to learn that Millán never had dreams. Dreams were extremely important to Borges. In a 1977 lecture, he admitted to having constant nightmares about labyrinths and mirrors and discussed with obvious approval the idea that dreams are the source of poetic inspiration. It would have been very difficult for him to share his inner life with someone whose mind did not summon up vivid images during the night.

Borges and his mother at the University of Texas in 1961. This was Borges's first trip to the United States, which he considered "the friendliest, most forgiving, and most generous nation I had ever visited." He and his mother even attended a football game and cheered for the Texas Longhorns.

Whatever the specific reasons, in 1970, Borges found himself back in his familiar, simply furnished room in the Maipú Street apartment. After his mother's death, he adjusted to a solitary life by organizing study groups at his home, giving lectures, talking with interviewers from all over the world, and taking part in literary events. From 1967 through 1972, he had worked closely with Norman Thomas di Giovanni to edit and collect many of his stories; di Giovanni had also acted as his agent in negotiations with publishers in various countries. As a result of these efforts, Borges enjoyed a comfortable income from the sale of his books and was able to live exactly as he pleased. In his case, this meant the ability to travel the world in spite of his blindness.

In 1976, Borges visited Japan as a guest of the Ministry of Education. The Far East had long fascinated him; during the 1930s, he had written a haunting story of loyalty and revenge entitled "The

Insulting Master of Etiquette Kôtsuké no Suké." In the story, he had evoked the atmosphere of 18th-century Japan solely through the power of his imagination. During his trip, he was able to understand the character of the country through his sense of hearing:

> Well, I attended a Kabuki play. It was a presentation of traditional Japanese music and dance. At the beginning, I confess, it seemed to me unbearable, especially the music, in which one cannot make out any melody. . . . But soon I started to get used to it, and finally I ended up attending the complete festival, which lasted, I believe, six or seven hours. During that time in the theater, one couldn't even hear a fly. . . . I am blind, and I remember that as I went in, I exclaimed, "Goodness, we are the only ones here." "No," my companion answered, "the room is full, Señor Borges." Nobody speaks loudly there. There may be a crowd, but if one doesn't see, as in my case, he may think that he is alone. Unquestionably, Japan is a civilized country; the most civilized I've ever known.

It was no coincidence that Borges chose to visit Japan at this time of his life. Among the students who attended the seminars at his

Borges sits in his mother's room, 9 years after her death at the age of 99. Borges had moved out of the apartment when he got married in 1967 but returned after his 1970 divorce. Following his mother's death, he relieved his solitude by organizing discussions and seminars at home.

home was María Kodama, an Argentine of Japanese ancestry. Having ended his association with Norman Thomas di Giovanni, Borges was in need of someone to handle his correspondence, and Kodama agreed to work part-time as his secretary. Before long, she began to help him care for himself and soon became his companion whenever he traveled.

In addition to being a pleasure in itself, travel also allowed Borges to escape from the continual stress of Argentine politics. In 1972, Juan Perón had returned from a 17-year exile in Spain. Peronism was still alive in Argentina, and Perón recaptured the presidency in 1973. This time, Perón had no power to harm Borges, who had become a folk hero in Argentina; his appearance in the street caused people to stop and stare and and exclaim to one another, "It's Borges!" According to Monegal, Borges's popularity with the Argentine masses was second only to that of Carlos Gardel, the legendary tango singer of the 1920s, whose recordings are like the national anthem to many Argentines. Nevertheless, Borges refused to serve a government headed by Perón and resigned as director of the National Library. As it turned out, Perón's second presidency was short-lived; he died in 1974, leaving the government in the hands of his third wife, Isabel, who was overthrown by another military coup in 1976.

Borges was severely tired of politics and resigned himself to tolerating the generals. "I suppose they are a necessary evil for the next 50 years or so," he was quoted as saying. He also remarked that the new president, General Jorge Rafael Videla, was basically a decent person. The government, eager to polish up its image, wanted Borges on its side and played up his tolerant attitude. However, Borges was certainly repelled when it became clear that the police and government-sponsored death squads had killed thousands of Argentines suspected of being Communists or terrorists. Borges supported the Mothers of the Plaza de Mayo, who demanded the exposure and punishment of these crimes, and he broke completely with the government over the disastrous Falk-

María Kodama helped Borges with his correspondence after his mother's death and eventually became his traveling companion. Here she accompanies Borges in Mexico City, which he visited in 1981 to receive Mexico's highest literary prize from President José López Portillo.

lands War of 1982. Nevertheless, his early association with the generals upset many liberals and leftists. It is easy to see why he frequently had the urge to leave Buenos Aires.

In a lavishly illustrated book entitled *Atlas*, published in 1984, Borges recounted with the help of María Kodama their travels throughout the world. There is an almost mythical element to the text and photos: The man who, as the writer Borges, encompassed the myths and literatures of all cultures now visits them as Borges the everyday person. It is as though he has found a magic carpet to take him to all the places he has summoned up in his dreams. He visits Rome; the ancient Greek theater at Epidaurus; stone monuments in Ireland; the great mosque of Istanbul; the canals of Venice; the labyrinth of Crete; the pyramids of Egypt; a temple in Japan. After dreaming of tigers all his life, he is finally able to touch one (presumably tame): "This tiger is of flesh and blood, and I arrived in its presence in a state of fearful felicity; its tongue licked my face and its indifferent or loving claw lingered atop my head. Unlike its precursors, this tiger was possessed of weight and odor." In Napa Valley, California, he arises at dawn to fly in a balloon.

> Space seemed unobstructed, and the unhurried wind, which carried us along as on a slow river, caressed our foreheads, our cheeks, the backs of our necks. I believe we all felt the same felicity, a felicity almost physical. I say *almost*, for there is no happiness or pain which is solely physical; the past always interposes itself. . . . The excursion, which must have lasted an hour and a half, was also a voyage through the lost paradise that is the nineteenth century.

Searching the past, he visits the Recoleta Cemetery in Buenos Aires. He finds the graves of his military ancestors, the graves of his

Among the many travel adventures Borges enjoyed during the 1980s was a balloon trip over the Napa Valley wine region in California. Although he could not enjoy the scenery, Borges delighted in the feel of the wind against his face and the sensation of traveling back through time.

parents, but concludes that *they* are not really there any more than *he* will be there. Like them, he will be "part of oblivion, the tenuous substance of which the universe is made."

On October 28, 1986, Jorge Luis Borges died of liver cancer in Geneva. After his work had become celebrated throughout the world, he had told an interviewer: "Through the years, a man peoples a space with images of provinces, kingdoms, mountains, bays, ships, islands, fishes, rooms, tools, stars, horses, and people. Shortly before his death, he discovers that the patient labyrinth of lines traces the image of his own face."

Those who have entered the labyrinth in search of Borges are unlikely ever to forget the image of his face.

Chronology

Aug. 24, 1899	Born Jorge Luis Borges in Buenos Aires, Argentina
1908	Translates Oscar Wilde's short story "The Happy Prince"
1914	Travels to Europe with his family; stranded in Switzerland due to the outbreak of World War I; attends high school at the Collège Calvin in Geneva
1920	Joins ultraist movement while in Spain
1921	Returns to Buenos Aires; introduces ultraism to Argentina
1921–30	Begins an intense period of writing, producing seven books; wins the Second Municipal Prize for *Cuaderno San Mártin*
1935	First short story collection, *A Universal History of Infamy*, is published
1936	Borges translates Virginia Woolf's *Room of One's Own*
1938	Father dies in February; Borges involved in a Christmas Eve accident, resulting in a

near-fatal illness; after recovery in 1939,
writes "Pierre Menard, Author of *Don Quixote*,"
which marks a breakthrough in his literary
development

1944   Publishes *Ficciones*, perhaps his best-known
collection of stories

1946   Juan Perón elected president of Argentina;
after criticizing government, Borges loses job
and is threatened with death; supports himself
by teaching and lecturing

1948   Mother and sister arrested for participation in
public demonstration against Perón regime

1955   Perón's regime is ousted; Borges named
director of National Library

1956   Becomes blind; appointed professor of
English and American literature at the
University of Buenos Aires; receives the
National Prize of Literature

1961   Shares International Publishers Prize with
Samuel Beckett; accepts position as visiting
professor at the University of Texas

1962   Work appears in English translation for first
time

1963   Borges travels through Europe

1967   Spends a year at Harvard University as visiting
professor of poetry; marries Elsa Astete Millán

1970   Borges and Millán divorce

1975	Borges's mother dies at the age of 99
1976	Borges visits Japan as a guest of the Ministry of Education
1982	Breaks with Argentine government over Falklands War against Great Britain
1986	Dies of liver cancer in Geneva

Further Reading

Agheana, Ian T. *The Meaning of Experience in the Prose of Jorge Luis Borges.* New York: Peter Lang, 1988.

Alazraki, Jaime. *Jorge Luis Borges.* New York: Columbia University Press, 1971.

Bell-Villada, Gene H. *Borges and His Fiction: A Guide to His Mind and Art.* Chapel Hill: University of North Carolina Press, 1981.

Bloom, Harold, ed. *Jorge Luis Borges.* New York: Chelsea House, 1986.

Borges, Jorge Luis. *The Aleph and Other Stories, 1933–1969.* Edited and translated by Norman Thomas di Giovanni in collaboration with the author. New York: Dutton, 1970.

———. *The Book of Sand.* Translated by Norman Thomas di Giovanni. New York: Dutton, 1977.

———. *Borges: A Reader.* Edited by Emir Rodriguez Monegal and Alastair Read. New York: Dutton, 1981.

———. *Doctor Brodie's Report.* Translated by Norman Thomas di Giovanni. New York: Dutton, 1971.

———. *Dreamtigers.* Translated by Mildred Boyer and Harold Morland. Austin: University of Texas Press, 1964.

———. *Ficciones.* Edited by Anthony Kerrigan. New York: Grove Press, 1962.

———. *Labyrinths: Selected Stories and Other Writings.* Edited by Donald A. Yates and James E. Irby. New York: New Directions, 1964.

———. *Other Inquisitions, 1937–1952.* Translated by Ruth L. C. Simms. Austin: University of Texas Press, 1964.

———. *A Personal Anthology.* Various translators. New York: Grove Press, 1967.

———. *Selected Poems, 1923–1967.* Edited by Norman Thomas di Giovanni. New York: Delacorte Press, 1972.

Burgin, Richard. *Conversations with Jorge Luis Borges.* New York: Holt, Rinehart & Winston, 1969.

Cheselka, Paul. *The Poetry and Poetics of Jorge Luis Borges.* New York: Peter Lang, 1987.

Cortinez, Carlos, ed. *Borges the Poet.* Fayetteville: University of Arkansas Press, 1986.

DeGaravalde, Giovanna. *Jorge Luis Borges: Sources and Illumination.* London: Octagonal Press, 1978.

Dunham, Lowell, and Ivar Ivask. *The Cardinal Points of Borges.* Norman: University of Oklahoma Press, 1971.

McMurray, George R. *Jorge Luis Borges.* New York: Ungar, 1980.

Monegal, Emir Rodriguez. *Jorge Luis Borges: A Literary Biography.* New York: Paragon House, 1978.

Sorrentino, Fernando. *Seven Conversations with Jorge Luis Borges.* Troy, NY: Whitson, 1981.

Sturrock, John. *Paper Tigers: The Ideal Fictions of Jorge Luis Borges.* New York: Oxford University Press, 1978.

Index

ADRIAN LENNON first studied Spanish at age five and was introduced to the works of Borges when he was nine. A lifelong resident of New York's Greenwich Village, a rabid sports enthusiast, and the author of several published mysteries, he is a devotee of Hispanic culture and history and has previously written a biography of Hernán Cortés.

RODOLFO CARDONA is professor of Spanish and comparative literature at Boston University. A renowned scholar, he has written many works of criticism, including *Ramón, a Study of Gómez de la Serna and His Works* and *Visión del esperpento: Teoría y práctica del esperpento en Valle-Inclán*. Born in San José, Costa Rica, he earned his B.A. and M.A. from Louisiana State University and received a Ph.D. from the University of Washington. He has taught at Case Western Reserve University, the University of Pittsburgh, the University of Texas at Austin, the University of New Mexico, and Harvard University.

JAMES COCKCROFT is currently a visiting professor of Latin American and Caribbean studies at the State University of New York at Albany. A three-time Fulbright scholar, he earned a Ph.D. from Stanford University and has taught at the University of Massachusetts, the University of Vermont, and the University of Connecticut. He is the author or coauthor of numerous books on Latin American subjects, including *Neighbors in Turmoil: Latin America*, *The Hispanic Experience in the United States: Contemporary Issues and Perspectives*, and *Outlaws in the Promised Land: Mexican Immigrant Workers and America's Future*.